LUFTWAFFE AT WAR

Stukas over the Mediterranean

Tethered to a large concrete block, this long range Ju 87-R *Stuka* sits on a Balkan airfield awaiting the move into Greece. The inscription on the radiator cowl reads 'Frostschutz Glykal'. *(Luftfahrtarchiv Griehl)*

LUFTWAFFE AT WAR

Stukas over the Mediterranean
1940–1945

Peter C. Smith

Greenhill Books
LONDON

Stackpole Books
PENNSYLVANIA

Greenhill Books

Dedicated to Richard P. Lutz and James V. Crow, for their very great help in the preparation of this book.

Stukas over the Mediterranean, 1940–1945
first published 1999 by Greenhill Books, Lionel Leventhal Limited, Park House, 1 Russell Gardens, London NW11 9NN
www.greenhillbooks.com
and
Stackpole Books, 5067 Ritter Road, Mechanicsburg, PA 17055, USA

British Library Cataloguing in Publication Data
Smith, Peter C. (Peter Charles), 1940-
Stukas over the Mediterranean, 1940-1945. - (Luftwaffe at war)
1. Germany. Luftwaffe - History 2. World War, 1939-1945 - Aerial operations, German 3. World War, 1939-1945 - Campaigns - Mediterranean Region
4. Stuka (Bombers) - History
I. Title
940.5'44'943

ISBN 1-85367-376-5

Library of Congress Cataloging-in-Publication Data
Smith, Peter Charles, 1940-
Stukas over the Mediterranean, 1940–1945/by Peter C. Smith.
  p.   cm. – (Luftwaffe at war; 11)
ISBN 1-85367-376-5
1. World War, 1939–1945 – Aerial operations, German. 2. World War, 1939–1945 – Campaigns – Mediterranean area. 3. Mediterranean Region – History, Military. 4. Stuka (Bombers). 5. Lightning war. I. Title. II. Series: Luftwaffe at war; v. 11.
D787.S598 1999   99-35086
940.54'4943–dc21   CIP

Designed by DAG Publications Ltd
Design by David Gibbons
Layout by Anthony A. Evans

Printed in Singapore

Right: A Ju 87B-2 with yellow radiator cowling is seen over the Mediterranean Sea in 1941. The transfer of German *Stuka* units was initially made late in 1940 with the specific intent of counteracting the Royal Navy's hold over the Italians. The *Stuka*s quickly proved their worth, damaging the aircraft carrier *Illustrious* with six direct hits and sinking the cruiser *Southampton* in January 1941. Support for the small military force of *General* Rommel's *Afrikakorps* followed and enabled him to re-occupy all the territory the British had won from the Italians in North Africa. With the invasion and occupation of Yugoslavia, Greece and Crete, the dominance of the *Stuka* in this new theatre of war was established. *(David Ethell)*

Below: This rare photograph is the only known colour picture of an Italian *Stuka*, a red spinnered Ju 87B with a white fuselage band. On the wheel spat is the abbreviated 'Diving Swan' emblem of 239 *Squadriglia*, 97 *Gruppo Bombardamento a Tuffo* (BaT) which was set up in November 1940, under *Tenente* Genni. It was based at the Lecce-Galatina airfield being concentrated in the Pigerasi area on 7 December, and they joined 96 *Gruppo* in attacks on Greek targets. *(Marco V. Bonelli)*

Left: *Major* Oskar Dinort, one of the most famous *Stuka* pilots and the *Geschwaderkommodore* of the St.G. 2 during the first two years of the war, stands on the non-slip walk strip of his aircraft after a mission. He wears the standard tan-coloured, overall canvas *Luftwaffe* summer flight suit. This was equipped with numerous zip pockets on the breast and legs, designed for easy access while in flight, with a large right-hand flap that buttoned down at the front. The large leather belt with metal buckle, and light-weight flying helmet with dark earphones, were typical flying gear for early Mediterranean operations in 1941. *(Herbert Léonard)*

Left: The cockpit of the two-seater *Stuka* was deliberately designed under a long canopy to give the pilot and rear-seat radio man and tail gunner the maximum vision necessary for dive bombing. This provided a good view, but made it vulnerable to attacking fighters, and later versions featured heavy armour plating and a streamlined canopy. In front of the pilot, on his frontal instrument panel, was the Revi reflector bomb aiming sight mounted on top of the grip bar. Note the straps of his parachute harness and the pilot's throat microphone. *(Herbert Léonard)*

Early in March 1941, the *Luftwaffe* moved into the Balkans to attack British forces in Greece, and the *Stuka* units based in Bulgaria and Romania were able to use the readily available airfields at Arad, Deta and Turnu Severin within days of arrival. When the pro-German government was overthrown in Belgrade, Yugoslavia was added to the list of matters to be dealt with and two additional *Stukagruppen* made the same journey from the channel coast of France, via Germany and south-eastern Europe to airfields in the extreme west of Romania, while another moved across from El Machin in Libya to Krainitz in Romania. *(Archiv Von Lutz)*

Yellow-nosed and tailed Berthas sit on a primitive Greek airstrip in April 1941. Within ten days some 120 *Stuka*s had been transferred from northern France to airfields in Bulgaria and Romania and then moved to hastily prepared airfields in Greece. *(Markus Richter)*

Right: The British and Commonwealth forces evacuated from Greece helped reinforce the island of Crete, already long utilised by the Royal Navy as a forward base against the Italians. *Generaloberst* Kurt Student, the AOC of *Fliegerkorps* XI Airborne troops, paratroopers and glider troops, gained Hitler's permission to take the island from the air as a seaborne invasion proved impracticable in the face of British sea power. Accordingly the *Stuka*s of *Fliegerkorps* VIII were moved forward to hastily prepared bases in southern Greece at Mulaoi, Melos and Scarpanto, as well as at Corinth and Argos. By the middle of May all was ready and the first massed formations of Junkers Ju 87Bs formed up and headed for the island to attack the defences. *(Harold Thiele)*

Below: In the fighting up and down the North African coast the *Stuka* units were in the thick of the action, being involved in the capture of Tobruk and attacks on Malta convoys as well as the retreat and the fighting against both British and the newly arrived American troops in Tunisia. Here the lean profile of a Dora of St.G. 1 is seen over the North African coast in 1942. *(Harold Thiele)*

Above: A badly beaten up 'Dora' discovered on a Sardinian airfield. It has been cannibalised for spares and has been the subject of a crash landing, as witnessed by the state of the propellers, but nonetheless the picture gives a good insight to the construction of this variant. The large supercharger air intake with its open cover can clearly be seen, as can undercarriage and leading wing edge detail. The tail carries the outlined swastika national emblem, but the front segment of both wheel spats are missing. *(David Ethell)*

Opposite page, top: The *Stuka*s that remained in Italy after the Sicily and Salerno invasions were soon split between the northern and southern sectors of that country, fighting either for Germany and the Fascist Italians or being taken over by the Allies, who did not use them operationally. After day-time operations against the Anzio beachhead in January 1944, the *Stuka* operations in the Mediterranean were increasingly taken over by the *Nachtschlacht* units, night harassment bombers which operated until almost the final months of the war, survivors of both types being evacuated to Germany in the final days. Here one such yellow-nosed *Nachtschlacht* Ju 87D (WerkNr. 141286) is seen at Fürth airfield being examined by American forces. Note the elongated flame-dampener exhaust led back over the wing and the absence of wheel spats, only the leather oleo covers remaining in situ. *(Archiv Von Lutz)*

Right: On a Greek airfield the Ju 87Bs of the 2./St.G. 2 'Immelmann' are lined up after making the transition to the Balkans in April, 1941. It was a feature of the *Luftwaffe*'s organisation that both combat units and their ground support staff were geared for such strategical and logistical moves as part of the main role in support of the Army. This, plus the German's internal lines of communication, made shifts of whole *Luftflotte*s a relatively swift exercise in comparison with cumbersome Allied methods around the periphery of Europe. *Stuka* units made the move within a few days of arriving, with 700 of their aircraft serviceable. *(Ken Merrick)*

Above: A Bertha-2 on a Balkan airfield in May 1941. The stubby mountings of the two MG-15 machine guns mounted on the leading edges of the wings can be clearly seen as can the large landing light. The spinner ring would seem to indi-cate this aircraft is from the 1./St.G. 77 which played a prominent part in the campaign against Yugoslavia and Greece. *(Ken Merrick)*

Left: Desert *Stuka*s. While 'Blackmen' – the mechanics nicknamed after their black overalls – work on the engine of a Junkers Ju 88 medium bomber on a primitive desert airstrip, two of the long-range *Stuka*s of the St.G. 1, with their underwing fuel tanks in place, stand amid drums of aviation fuel on the perimeter of the run-way. There is no attempt at concealment, indicating that fear of retaliation is slight, nor is there any camouflage netting in view. Nor is there, as yet, any attempt to change the standard *Luftwaffe* paint scheme, although that was soon to alter. *(Ken Merrick)*

Above: The combat career of the Junkers Ju 87 *Stuka* can almost be said to have started in the Mediterranean, for it was with the *Legion Kondor* of German 'volunteers' fighting in Spain, on the side of the Nationalist leader General Franco, that the famous dive bomber made its debut. Here is seen one of the early Antons in Nationalist markings. *(Archiv Schliephake)*

Below: The *Kette* of Berthas K/88, which was formed from the five Ju 87Bs shipped out from Germany in 1938 to replace the Antons, operated from La Cenia airfield during the advance on Valencia, on Spain's Mediterranean Golfo de Valencia in the spring of 1938. The port facilities and shipping in the docks at Valencia, Barcelona and Tarragona were all found to be perfect targets for dive bombing and great havoc was caused by their attacks. *(Archiv Schliephake)*

Top left: Hitler's Italian allies entered the war in June 1940, thinking it was almost over and hoping to obtain easy pickings without too much effort. However they soon found that the Royal Navy in the Mediterranean was more than a match for their own Navy and the British Army in Egypt equally the match of their Army. After several humiliating defeats at sea and in the desert Hitler lost patience and dispatched a small land force under *General* Erwin Rommel to rectify the situation and, at the same time, dispatched a special dive bomber task force under *General der Flieger* Geisler to Sicily to deal with the Royal Navy. These are Berthas of St.G. 2 'Immelmann' with their tarpaulin covers over the engine and cockpit. *(Franz Selinger)*

Above: The II./St.G. 2 under *Major* Walter Enneccerus and 1./St. G. 1 under *Hauptmann* Paul-Werner Hozzel, both anti-shipping specialists, were sent out to Sicily with instructions from Hitler himself, whose directive ordered '*Illustrious* must be sunk'. The British carrier had carried out several sweeps. In October 1940 her torpedo bombers had sunk three of Italy's six battleships anchored in their main base at Taranto, another major humiliation for the Italians. The *Stuka*s were to rectify this and they practised bombing a floating mock-up of the carrier anchored off the Sicilian coast. This is a line-up of St.G. 2 Berthas with their famous 'Scottie' dog emblem. *(Franz Selinger)*

Left: Under the anti-shipping specialist, *Oberst* Martin Harlinghausen, acting as Chief-of-Staff to *General der Flieger* Hans Ferdinand Geisler, *Fliegerkorps* X was soon established on Catania and Comiso, Sicily. The two *Stuka* units of that command, II./St.G. 2 and I./St.G. 2 were training hard in readiness to strike at the British Mediterranean Fleet and especially the aircraft carrier *Illustrious*. In January 1941 the British sailed into the Sicilian Straits to cover a convoy to Malta and Alexandria. This a Ju 87d of St.G. 2 with her Shamrock emblem returning from a sortie. *(Archiv Von Lutz)*

Above: The 23,000-ton aircraft carrier HMS *Illustrious* was the first to be equipped with an armoured deck for protection from bombs of up to 500 lb. It had already made its mark in the Mediterranean with the famous attack on Taranto which destroyed half of Mussolini's battleship force at a stroke, and was the prime target of *Fliegerkorps* X's dive bombers. *Illustrious* is seen here leaving Alexandria harbour to take part in Operation EXCESS, the passage of a convoy through the Sicilian Channel close to the *Stukas*' main Italian airfields. *(E.B. Mackenzie)*

Below: 10 January 1941 and *Illustrious* is attacked south of Sicily by the Stukas of *Fliegerkorps* X. While Italian Sm 79 torpedo bombers approaching low lured away her defending Fairey Fulmar fighters, and some of the Junkers Ju 87s attacked the escorting battleships *Warspite* and *Valiant* to occupy their anti-aircraft batteries, the bulk of the *Stukas* concentrated on the carrier. This photograph shows a near miss off the carrier's bows, while the attacking *Stuka* can be seen (top right) pulling out of her dive at a low level. *(Imperial War Museum)*

Right: The scene aboard *Illustrious* in the immediate aftermath of the *Stuka* attack on 10 January 1941. Looking aft from the ship's bridge the smoke from internal fires in the hangar decks below seeps up between the armour deck plating, while the damaged after lift can be seen canted up at an angle. Hit by one bomb while on the way down, the ship was struck by a second bomb which went down and exploded among the parked aircraft below. Amazingly the ship's engine rooms were unharmed and she was able to keep steaming. *(Imperial War Museum)*

Right: A postscript to the *Illustrious* attack on 10 January 1941. The two young *Stuka* pilots (centre front in overalls and with head bandaged behind naval rating), seen here with a naval escort, were shot down over the fleet and subsequently rescued by an escorting British destroyer. *(E.B. Mackenzie)*

Left: The Italian *'Stuka'*. After the success of the Junkers Ju 87 in Spain, Mussolini demanded that the *Regia Aeronautica* equip itself with such an aircraft. The subsequent *Stato Maggiore dell' Aeronautica* plan, 'Programme R' of 1940, called for a single seater dive bomber able to carry a 500 kg bomb with an airframe strong enough to withstand dives of between 40 and 90 degrees. Alessandro Marchetti started design work to this specification and the SIAI Sm 85 dive bomber was the result. This twin-engined aircraft was built with a wooden box airframe and had a cantilever wing and retractable landing gear. To offer good downward visibility the fuselage was marked by a distinctive upward sweep to both nose and tail, and the bomb was carried internally. The first prototype flew on 19 December 1936, but proved to be under powered. *(Nicola Malizia)*

Lower left: Two further views of the first Italian dive bomber produced specifically to imitate the success of the Junkers Ju 87. The Sm 85 was powered by two 460 hp Piaggio PV11 engines and was a wooden machine, like most Italian aircraft of this period. Despite Marchetti's plans the Sm 85 proved a disappointment. Its unique upswept fuselage shape earned it the sobriquet 'Flying Banana', but its subsequent aeronautical performance could equally merit that title. Being designed exclusively for dive bombing the single seater cockpit was set forward over the short nose to

provide a good forward view. Their main targets were to be the ships of the Royal Navy's Mediterranean Fleet, the main opposition to Mussolini's towering ambitions in the area and trials against moving warship targets were conducted. *(Aeronautica Militare Ult DOC e A.P.)*

Below: The SIAI Sm 85 was placed into limited production following two further test S85 test aircraft had been trialled in March and April 1937, with modifications to the cockpit and some thirty-six of the type were built, the first of which joined the experimental dive bomber unit. These tests proved that the aircraft was just not up to the job, but as Mussolini insisted on a dive bomber squadron, one was duly formed, 96° *Gruppo Bombardamento a Tuffo* (BaT) which was established on 20 March, 1940 with two *Squadriglie* (236 and 237) totalling eighteen Sm 85s and one Sm 86. Just before Italy joined the war, this unit was based on Pantellaria Island, arriving on 5 June 1940. They only took part in one combat sortie against the Royal Navy's Mediterranean Fleet, during the Battle of Calabria on 19 July, but they failed to even find the British warships and the mission was totally abortive. The damp, humid conditions at Pantellaria wrought havoc with the wooden aircraft and shortly afterwards they were withdrawn as being unserviceable, and later were all scrapped. *(Aeronautica Militare Ult DOC e A.P.)*

Right: In an attempt to improve the performance of the Sm 85, Alessandro Marchetti tried to incorporate the harsh lessons learned from the tests. The new design the Sm 86, featured the more powerful Walter Sazitta 600 hp engines, driving three-bladed, variable-pitch propellers and a generally cleaned-up fuselage and wing form. The first prototype, pictured here, first flew on 8 April 1939. On 10 May 1940 it was transferred to the 1° *Centro Sperimentale* at Guidonia, and they reported the aeroplane was unsatisfactory for the job as a dive bomber. *(Aeronautica Militare Ult DOC e A.P.)*

Below and lower right: The failure of the Sm 85 and Sm 86 designs of home grown dive bombers forced the Italians to turn to their German allies for help. Several batches of *Stuka*s were purchased outright and Italian fighter pilots were selected to hastily train as dive bomber pilots in Germany. This did not prevent the Italian aircraft industry from attempting to both convert existing aircraft to dive bombing, or design from scratch new dive bombers, none of which came to anything other than a few prototypes. Among the new types that resulted was the Caproni Ca 335 seen in these three photographs. Only the German built and supplied *Stuka*s went into battle for Mussolini. *(Nicola Malizia)*

Opposite page, top: After he had studied in full the details of the Sm 85 failure *Generale* Francesco Pricolo, the Chief of the Italian Air Staff, dispatched a special mission to Germany. The outcome was an initial agreement for Italy to purchase batches of both Berthas and the long-range Richard types of the Junkers Ju 87 for their own use, and for fifteen selected Italian pilots to be trained in Germany to form the first dive bomber unit. Here a trio of Italian pilots is seen undergoing flight training at Graz, Austria, the pilot of the aircraft in the foreground being Giuseppe Cenni, later to become the foremost Italian dive bomber ace. *(Cesare Gori)*

Left: The *Stuka* was never manufactured in Italy and the aircraft arrived there still bearing their German national insignia and other markings, which had to be replaced with Italian national and unit insignia. They were converted for work in the North African desert with sand filters and survival equipment. July 1940 saw the first Italian pilot training commenced at Graz, and by 21 August 1940 they started to re-equip 96° *Gruppo*, with 236 and 237 *Squadriglie*, at Comiso airfield in Sicily for attacks on Malta. The Italians nicknamed the Stuka the *'Picchiatelli'* ('striker') and they were soon in action. *(Nicola Patella)*

Above: Although the initial training of Italian *Stuka* aircrew was conducted at a crash course in Graz, subsequent dive bomber training on the type was moved to Italy. Here is a Ju 87 of the *Scuola Tuffatori* (Dive Bomber School) flying over Lombardy. At this period the school was based at Lonate Pozzo airfield. The increased size of the aircraft's fuselage band indicates that this is a machine from the Italian training school. *(I. Acquarelli via Nicola Malizia)*

Above: A tethered Italian *Stuka* undergoing engine maintenance at Comiso airfield on Sicily in 1941. This is an obviously posed shot, with the man in the centre working a hand pump to refuel the starboard wing tank from drums of aviation fuel. The engineers working on the aircraft would get in each other's way in practice, but the photograph affords a good view of the *Stuka*'s parts forward of the cockpit. *(Marco V. Bonelli)*

Below: Despite wide differences in many spheres of the war, the Germans and the Italians co-operated well in the air war at the start. *Stuka*s of both air forces took part in combined attacks against objectives such as Malta's harbours and airfields and British army positions in Egypt throughout 1941. Here an Italian Fiat G-50 Freccia fighter provides close escort for a German Ju 87 of the II./St.G. 1. *(Schneider via James V. Crow)*

Above: With the ill-judged and ultimately disastrous decision by Mussolini to invade Greece in the winter of 1940 from occupied Albania, the Italians were drawn into another humiliating military disaster. Initial advances were first halted and then thrown back and the invasion turned into a rout. To give what aid they could the Italian *Stuka*s were transferred to Lecce in November and had to contend with snow, blizzards and primitive conditions as well as tough Greek opposition. Here 208 *Squadriglia*, which with 209 *Squadriglia* had joined the fray in March 1941, returns from a mission with empty bomb cradles. *(Marco V. Bonelli)*

Below: The main German *Stuka* operations for the first three months of 1941 continued to be the support of the *Afrikakorps* against the British in Libya and Malta, and attacks on British supply convoys attempting to lift the blockade from either Gibraltar in the west or Alexandria in the east. The Royal Navy decided it was inadvisable to venture into the Sicilian 'narrows' with heavy warships unless it was entirely necessary and set up so called '*Stuka* Sanctuaries', areas thought to be beyond the reach of the Ju 87 in which they operated with relative immunity. This served the Navy as long as the *Stuka*'s North African coastal airstrips were kept in Libya and the Balkan coast to the north remained friendly or neutral, but those conditions were not maintained. Here two long range Richards of the II./St.G. 3 are seen over Benghazi. *(Archiv Von Lutz)*

Left: With the basing of dive bomber units in Sicily, improvements began to be made by the ground teams to protect the *Stuka*s from the worst of the heat and dust. They were converted by the fitting of sand filters etc. and base facilities were also improved. Here a Italian *Stuka* revetment is under construction on a Sicilian airfield with poles and brushwood serving both as wind protection and partial camouflage. *(Marco V. Bonelli)*

Below: An Italian *Stuka* aircrew from the 209 *Squadriglia* poses for the camera on a Sicilian airfield. On the left is *Sergente Maggiore* Tarantola Ennio with, on his right, 1o *Aviatore Fotogratio* (Aerial Photographer) Ricci. Their flying outfits make an interesting comparison with those of their *Luftwaffe* cousins as represented by Oskar Dinort (see colour section). *(Nicola Malizia)*

Above: Before the planned attack on Greece could take place, the Yugoslav government, friendly to Germany, was overthrown in a *coup d'etat*. Hitler vowed to bring that country to heel and hasty planning included the attack on Yugoslavia in conjunction with the attack on Greece. The Yugoslav government thought that the Germans would need several months before they could mount any operations but, within less than a week, Germany had further

reinforcements flown in and was ready to open hostilities. Here are members of the *Stab* (Staff) unit of the St.G. 77 on Arad airfield in Romania in April 1941 enjoying the sunshine just before the assault. From left to right: *Staffelkapitän Oberleutnant* Georg Jakob, with officers Schongarth, Otto Schmidt, Horst Kaubisch and Alexander Glaser. *(Sellhorn Archiv)*

Left: The horse-drawn columns of the Yugoslav Army were shattered by the attacks of the *Stuka/Panzer* combination and within a few days had been defeated in the south and east of the country, pulling back for a last stand in the capital Belgrade. The Yugoslavs relied on natural lines of defence to delay the Germans. Pancevo was targeted by St.G. 77. on the way to Belgrade. Here the River Danube was reached in April 1941 and on the right of the photograph is the wrecked road bridge into the capital itself. On the left German engineers are constructing a pontoon bridge across from both banks to replace it. *(Schobert via Sellhorn Archiv)*

Above: *Stuka* over the Danube, Belgrade 1941. Within a few days the Germans had defeated the Yugoslav Army in the south and centre of the country and were pressing hard on the capital city. *(Franz Selinger Archiv)*

Below: The main road bridge into the city of Belgrade itself was demolished. Under the wing of a Ju 87B of the I./St.G. 77 can be seen a new pontoon bridge being constructed by German engineers. Note the short muzzled MG-17 wing machine gun, fitted without a flash muzzle on this particular aircraft. *(Sellhorn Archiv)*

Opposite page, top: Despite the change of government, not all the Yugoslav population was anti-German. Many supported the occupation initially if it meant the overthrow of their political enemies. Here personnel of the I./St.G. 77 are greeted by the local populace at a village near their base of Bijeljina in the north-western part of the country on 15 April 1941. The four crewmen in this photograph with the village girls are, from left to right, Flight Leader *Unteroffizier* Paul Langkopf; Flight Leader *Feldwebel* Willi Knauer; Radioman *Feldwebel* Walter Muller and Radioman *Unteroffizier* Ernest Maurer. *(Gramlich via Sellhorn Archiv)*

Opposite page, bottom: The *Stuka* of *Oberleutnant* Rudolf Neumann, who was flying with the 3. *Staffel* St.G. 77 at Semlin airfield Belgrade after its occupation. Note the commander's metal pennant mounted on the cockpit of the aircraft, which is undergoing engine maintenance. *(Sellhorn Archiv)*

Opposite page, top: Arad in Romania, the original base of the I./St.G. 77 in the Balkans campaign, 6 April 1941. *Feldwebel* Paul Klose, an aircraft radio fitter, is seated on an SC 250 bomb, under the wing of the *Stuka* belonging to the Adjutant, *Oberleutnant* Karl Henze. Note the spinner on the 'Trumpet of Jericho' wind-driven siren. *(Oelschlager via Sellhorn Archiv)*

Above: Heading out on another mission across the Struma River, these Berthas with yellow noses and rudders and full bomb loads belong to St.G. 77. *(Wilhelm Landau, via James V. Crow)*

Left: Not all the *Stuka* units carried the yellow paint identification: some were in action before this could be applied. Here a *Kette* of fully armed Bertha-2s from the St.G. 3 take off from their forward grass airstrip during the Yugoslav campaign in April 1941. *(Archiv Von Lutz)*

Top left: The primitive conditions encountered in the Balkans during the brief spring campaign showed what could be expected for the forthcoming operations against the Soviet Union. Here a *Kette* of Berthas from the St.G. 3 are seen flying to the combat zone with the wheel spats removed. *(Archiv Von Lutz)*

Left: The surrender of the 2nd Serbian Army by parley at the base airfield of the I./St.G. 77 at Bijeljina, northern Yugoslavia, to the west of Belgrade. Third on the right is the *Oberwerkmeister* of the 2. *Staffel*, *Oberfeldwebel* Hackbath. *(Oelschlager via Sellhorn Archiv)*

Above: This Ju 87-R of the I./St.G. 3 in the Balkans has the whole of its tail section and nose painted yellow (the *Staffel* colour), with the square containing the swastika left in the original green. The 'C' of the fuselage identification letters is also yellow. *(Willi Tritsch, via James V. Crow)*

Below: This Bertha of the I./St.G. 77 shows a wholly different interpretation of the combat zone markings for the Balkan campaign, the yellow tail being confined to the rudder only, while there is a broad band only around the nose. This is the aircraft of the *Gruppenkommandeur*, Hauptman Bruck, with his radioman, *Feldwebel* Muller, seen over Greece. *(Sellhorn Archiv)*

Above: The 'Blackmen' hard at work on the engine of a St.G. 2 Bertha. Notice that the two wind-driven sirens on the undercarriage legs have had their propellers removed, and their fairing caps are in place, as are those on the two machine gun fairings on the wings. Outboard of the dive brake a pair of small 110 kg bombs are already in place. The nose and tail are painted yellow for the Balkans operation. *(Author's collection)*

Below: The upturned radiator cowling of a Bertha forms an impromptu frame for this mechanic of the St.G. 2 during the brief Balkans campaign of April–May 1941. In the background serviced units stand near the tented encampment of the hastily prepared airfields with tarpaulins in place over engines and cockpits to keep out the heat and dust between missions. *(Author's collection)*

Above: A strong formation of yellow nosed Junkers Ju 87Bs crosses the southern coastal mountains of Greece *en route* to deliver attacks on British positions around Maleme airfield, Crete, in dive bombing raids that paved the way for the German airborne assault of May 1941. *(Franz Selinger)*

Below: The docks at Salamis and elsewhere on the Greek southern coast were dive bombed during the brief assault that overcame the Greek army and forced the British forces from defensive positions until evacuated by the Royal Navy. Here is a tail gunner's view of a *Stuka* attack on British motor transport awaiting embarkation at an Adriatic port. *(Author's collection)*

Above: The *Stuka*s suffered few losses during the brief campaigns which overran Yugoslavia and Greece and these were mainly from anti-aircraft fire. Here are a trio of *Stuka* victims, damaged Berthas on the edge of Larissa airfield, Greece, stripped down and awaiting transportation back to Germany for full repair. *(A.D. Chapman)*

Below: The Royal Navy's only heavy cruiser in the Eastern Mediterranean at this period of the war was HMS *York*, seen here leaving Alexandria harbour. This was destined to be the most powerful warship destroyed by the Junkers Ju 87 up to that date. *(E.B. Mackenzie)*

Opposite page, top: In addition to the warships sunk by the *Stuka*s off Crete in May 1941, many more were hit and damaged. Among them was the aircraft carrier *Formidable* seen here on arrival in the Mediterranean in February. On 25 May, the ship was attacked off Crete by a group of twenty Junkers 87s led by *Major* Walter Enneccerus of the II./St.G. 2 which scored two direct hits on the carrier. *(E.B. Mackenzie)*

Opposite page, bottom: One of the hits on the aircraft carrier *Formidable* on 25 May 1941, south of Crete, blew out a whole section of the starboard side plating below the armoured flight deck forward. This is the view from inside the carrier showing the extent of the damage. *(E.D. Wilson via Fleet Air Arm Museum, Yeovilton)*

Above: A *Stuka* of 239 *Squadriglia*, 97° *Gruppo* of the Italian Air Force returning from a mission over Tobruk in the summer of 1941. By now the *Stuka* training programme was bearing fruit and more and more Italian dive bomber units were coming into service. *(Nicola Malizia)*

Below: Although fewer in number than their German counterparts, the Italian *Stuka* units, formed mainly with former fighter pilots, began to throw up their own aces. Although trained in the German manner, the individuality and flair of the Italians was allowed full reign and some, like *Major* Giuseppe Cenni pictured here driving the towing tractor that was hauling his own aircraft along the runway at Comiso, Sicily, began to formulate their own unique ideas. 'Skip bombing', long hailed as an American anti-ship invention and used in the Battle of the Bismarck Sea in the Pacific in 1942, was actually invented the year before by Cenni and his unit using the *Stuka* dive bomber. *(Cesare Gori)*

Above: Italian dive bombers in action. *Stuka*s from 239 *Squadriglia*, led by *Major* Giuseppi Cenni, swarm over the British gunboat HMS *Cricket* off the North African coast. *(Cesare Gori)*

Below: Although the German dive bombers sent to work from dusty airstrips in the North African desert were converted, working conditions were far from ideal. The Junkers Ju 87 had been built for just such rough and ready front line conditions and the fixed undercarriage came into its own in such conditions proving to be both sturdy and reliable. Here a *Stuka* returning from a mission kicks up a minor sand storm in its wake as it comes in to land. *(Robert Michulec)*

Left: German *Stuka*s took part in attacks on Tobruk, which was held under siege for about a year when the main German thrust eastward along the North African coast by-passed it. Here another pair of Junkers Ju 87Bs takes off from the forward base to attack the area once again, watched by the ground crew working on another aircraft. *(Hanfried Schliephake)*

Above: Preparing for take-off, the rear-seat radio operator and tail gunner assists his pilot with his straps as they board their Ju 87B. This aircraft is of the 5./St.G. 2 (coded T6 + EN, WerkNr. 56722) and carries that unit's emblem on its forward fuselage. The oval slot above the badge is the flare pistol aperture, the rear-seat man is standing on the non-slip strip of the central wing section and is wearing standard *Luftwaffe* parachute and harness. *(James V. Crow)*

Below: A *Kette* of Berthas lifts off from a Cyrenaican airfield. Even in pre-war Italian airfields like this one, facilities were relatively civilised. The long line of trees planted in the background as a break from the dust storms of the region helped, but they were never free of the sand. Camouflage netting shields a bomb dump, but there was little fear of retaliatory strikes at this stage of the war and bombs are scattered around the airfield perimeter. In the background further *Stuka*s can be seen taking off (centre left) or moving onto the runway in readiness (centre right). *(James V. Crow)*

Above: A long range Ju 87R over the Mediterranean. This one is the mount of *Major* Enneccerus and carries the *Afrikakorps* insignia on its nose. *(US National Archives, College Park, MD)*

Below: Scrub, dust and sand, a Ju 87R-2 taxies across a forward desert air strip close to the front line. As well as special dust filters, converted *Stuka*s were fitted with desert survival kit, extra rations, knives, spades, compass, water bottles etc, as the chances of escaping from the desert in the event of a forced landing were often bleak, the aircrew having to cope with unfriendly Bedouin tribes, British long range patrols and the natural hazards of the area as well as the heat of the day and the intense cold of the night. *(Archiv Von Lutz)*

Above: Returning from a mission and flying over a typical North African landscape of scrub and sand, this is a long range Ju 87R freshly painted in desert colour, sand yellow (RLM 79) topsides and light blue (RLM 65) undersurfaces. The fuselage band is white, as are the extreme lower wing tips. The spinner is yellow and the black national markings are silhouetted in white. *(E.J. Creek via Archiv Von Lutz)*

Below: A *Kette* from the St.G. 2 land in unison on a desert air strip after another sortie. The camouflage is now a mixture of the original black-green (RLM 70) and sand yellow (RLM 79) in a mottled pattern over the upper surfaces, with the standard light blue (RLM 65) being retained on lower surfaces. The wing tips are painted white, as was the band around the after fuselage, although not visible in this shot. They had red spinners with a green tip and a white stripe, while the national markings on wings and tail were still outlined in white, and as can be clearly seen in this close-up of the port wing, were the original markings which were painted around. *(Alain Fleuret via Archiv Von Lutz)*

Above: Initially, not all the *Stuka*s transferred to the Mediterranean theatre of operations (MTO) were camouflaged in desert colours, as many operated from either Sicily or Greece. Here are pictured the fully bombed-up Ju 87D-2s of the 4./St.G. 2 heading out over the North African coast in late 1941. They still carry a mix of black-green (RLM 70) paint on their upper surfaces, with light blue (RLM 65) lower surfaces and white tips to their spinners. Their only concession to their new role at this stage is the *Afrikakorps* insignia on the noses. *(Archiv Von Lutz)*

Top right: The *Stuka* was designed and built exclusively as a dive bomber and its natural position was nose down. One thing that the Junkers Ju 87 was notorious for was the 'Kopfstand', a nose-up landing which buckled many a

propeller, and the primitive forward airfields of the North African desert made such undignified terminations all the more likely. Usually the damage suffered was slight and was soon repaired. This time the culprit is a Bertha-2 of the 2./St.G. 3. *(Archiv Von Lutz)*

Right: A Richard on the hunt off the Libyan Coast early in 1942. The long range fuel tanks gave these aircraft the extra mileage to attack the convoys making their way to Malta with supplies, fuel and reinforcements. As Rommel drove the British back beyond the Libyan/Egyptian border, the *Stuka*s with their extra range were able to strike at the British fleet further east. *(US National Archives, College Park, MD)*

Above: The other main role for the Sicilian based *Stuka*s, often transferred from the Russian Front for periods specifically for the job, was the subjugation of the island fortress of Malta. Although bombed continually since June 1940, the island had not been put out of action as an air and naval base. Royal Navy surface ships and submarines, assisted by Royal Navy and RAF torpedo bombers, had proved a thorn in the side of the Axis by cutting and disrupting Rommel's vital oil tanker and supply ship routes from Italy to Libya. During 1941 the *Luftwaffe* mounted an series of attacks, initially triggered by the need to eliminate the carrier *Illustrious* which was docked there, but gradually extended to cover all the airfields on the island as well. Initially the island had little or no fighter protection other than a few Gloster Gladiator biplanes and relied for its defence on anti-aircraft guns. Here Hal Far airfield is seen under the wing tip of a *Stuka* which is circling to make her dive. *(Hanfried Schliephake)*

Left: Flak damage was heavy especially when the *Stuka*s attacked targets in Valetta harbour, which was protected by a ring of guns that grew steadily as the war went on and more supply convoys reached the island. Eventually each inlet of the harbour was ringed with 20 mm Oerlikon and 40 mm Bofors light anti-aircraft positions. This photograph shows the result of a flak hit on the starboard wing of Helmut Mahlke, who managed to fly his aircraft back to his base in Sicily. *(Archiv Schliephake)*

Right: Despite flak damage sustained during their dive bombing attacks over Valetta harbour, many *Stuka*s managed to survive to return more or less intact to their Sicilian bases. As in Poland, the sturdiness of the little bomber and the stoutness of her construction often saved her aircrew. This photo shows the hole made by a shell that ripped through the port wing of this Bertha just abaft the two wing bomb carriers. It also affords a good view of the internal wing structure composition and the slatted dive brake. *(Archiv Schliephake)*

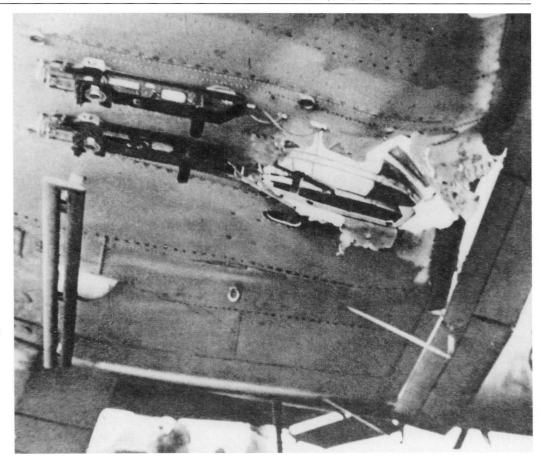

Right: The *Stuka*s of the *Regia Aeronautica* played their full part in the blitz on Malta. This tranquil scene shows a pair of Junkers Ju 87B-2s of the 102° *Gruppo*, of 5° *Stormo Tuffatori*. They are on the way to the home base of Gela, Sicily. *(Nicola Malizia)*

Top left: A portrait of a formation of Junkers Ju 87R-2s of the 208 *Squadriglia* of 101º *Gruppo*, 5º *Stormo Tuffatori* returning to their airfield at Trapani Milo in Sicily after an attack on Malta. To the left can be seen the distinctive Monte Erice. *(A. Coppola via Nicola Malizia)*

Bottom left: Fresh Italian *Stuka* crews continued to be trained once their initial success was found to be sustainable and batches of newer Junkers Ju 87s were purchased. The training was moved from Graz, Austria, to bases in mainland Italy itself. Here a quartet of newly qualified aircrew is seen during a practice flight over Lombardy, the aircraft tail nearest the camera carrying the Italian batch number MM 7071 at the top in front of the national insignia. *(Nicola Patella)*

Above: The Italian *Stuka* units operated over the Libyan coast attacking British and Allied ships conveying supplies into Tobruk during the siege. This is 239 *Squadriglia* returning from one such mission. *(Nicola Malizia)*

Below: Another victim of the Italian *Stukas*: an undefended Allied freighter attacked close inshore off Corfu. Beneath the port wing tip of a Ju 87 the hole in the ship's side caused by one of the bombs can be seen. *(Nicola Malizia)*

Above: Not all shipping targets were undefended. Here 239 *Squadriglia* is seen diving through anti-aircraft fire to attack an Allied convoy located off the coast of Libya. *(Nicola Malizia)*

Below: Their attack successfully completed, the Ju 87B-2s of 239 *Squadriglia* reform and with empty bomb crutches swaying in their slip streams, head back along the coast to the base. *(Nicola Malizia)*

Above: A *Kette* of *Stuka*s swoops low over men of the *Deutsches Afrikakorps* (DAK) in the North African desert on completion of a close support mission in 1942. *(Imperial War Museum, London)*

Below: As 1942 wore on the British fighter defences became stronger and began to affect *Stuka* operations. During the final attempt by Rommel to break through the last defensive line before Cairo and the Suez Canal his *Stuka*s were thrown into the cauldron and losses inevitably mounted. In this remarkable photograph the final moments of a *Stuka* are caught on camera as it crashes in the desert, victim of an Allied Curtiss Kittyhawk attack. *(Illustrated London News Picture Library)*

Left: Several *Stuka*s fell victim to Allied fighters during the final drive on Cairo. Here a dazed, shirt-sleeved, rear-seat man of a *Stuka* that crash-landed behind Allied lines during the summer of 1942 is taken prisoner by an officer. *(Illustrated London News Picture Library)*

Lower left: By far the largest of all the Malta convoys was Operation PEDESTAL, mounted from the western end of the Mediterranean between 10 and 14 August 1942. Four fleet aircraft carriers were involved, *Furious*, *Eagle*, *Indomitable* and *Victorious*, along with two battleships, seven cruisers and twenty-nine destroyers, providing escort for fourteen merchant ships attempting to run the gauntlet of the Sicilian narrows. Beset by all forms of attack by Axis surface warships and submarines and both German and Italian dive bombers and torpedo bombers, the convoy suffered grievously. Only four of the merchant ships, plus the solitary tanker, *Ohio*, all damaged, finally reached Malta. This photo shows the *Stuka*s of the I./St.G. 3 led by *Hauptmann* Martin Mossdorf attacking the aircraft carrier *Indomitable*. *(Imperial War Museum, London)*

Below: As the summer of 1942 wore on the plight of Malta became more and more desperate and attempts to fight through supply convoys became more and more hazardous. This photo shows the view astern as a *Stuka* pulls out of her dive over the Australian manned destroyer *Nestor*. Bomb hits can be seen on the ship fore and aft. *(Author's collection)*

Above: A Ju 87R-2 of the *Stab* flight of the St.G. 2 'Immelmann'. The *Stabkette* insignia of white cross upon a black shield can be clearly seen on the forward fuselage, while the 'Trumpet of Jericho' wind sirens have been capped off at this period. The individual aircraft letter 'C' is also carried on each of the wheel spats. *(Archiv Von Lutz)*

Left: In the retreat in North Africa that followed the El Alamein battle in October 1942, the few remaining *Stuka*s had to be pulled back as the DAK and its Italian allies were bundled out of Egypt and Libya. By this time the Italian *Stuka* units had been mainly withdrawn to Sicily and Italy to recoup and replenish. Fresh batches had been ordered from Germany to replace the worn out Berthas and Richards that had carried on the fight for three years. Always the demands of Eastern Front had the priority and the Ju 87D came late to the desert war. Here two Italian *Stuka* pilots of 102° *Gruppo* are pictured on a Sicilian airfield after taking part in combat sorties against Malta convoy PEDESTAL in August 1942. *(Author's collection)*

Above: The Anglo-American landings in Vichy North Africa confined the remaining German forces to a tiny area of Tunis, hemmed in from all sides. Only twenty to thirty German *Stuka*s remained, operating from concrete runways or roads to attack Allied land forces. This is a Dora-3 of the 3./St.G. 3 in Tunisia, March 1943, stuck in the mud with Arabs pressed in to help dig it out. *(Archiv Von Lutz)*

Below: A Ju 87R with very distinctive camouflage pattern on a Tunisian airfield in late 1942 or early 1943. Hopelessly outnumbered by huge numbers of Allied fighters, the German dive bombers survived by staying on the ground until patrols withdrew and then carried out fast, efficient attacks before they could be caught. *(James V. Crow)*

Above: The pilot and some friends gather round this Dora of the 7./St.G. 1 in Tunisia in 1943, to examine the hole left by an anti-aircraft shell hit over the front, which has peeled back the side panelling of the *Stuka* without damaging any of its vitals. *(Archiv Von Lutz)*

Right: During the final weeks of the Tunisian campaign the German High Command finally seemed to realise the importance of holding the North African coast, and, after three years of virtually starving the theatre of men and equipment, started to fly in all manner of reinforcements to the Tunisian bridgehead. Gliders were used to ferry in troops, but these slow and vulnerable units were easy prey for Allied fighter patrols and suffered accordingly. Some *Stuka*s had been fitted out as glider tugs, with a sturdy tail box welded to the underside of the rear fuselage to hold a glider tug for the towing cable. This photo shows a *Stuka* and troop glider of the 7.II./LLG. 1 in the Balkans in 1944. *(Helmut Mahr via James V. Crow)*

Above: The end in Tunisia could not be delayed for ever, and when it came all serviceable *Stuka*s escaped to Sicily. Inevitably there were many damaged, or undergoing repair, that had to be abandoned to their fate, and thus the Allies were able to study several abandoned variants at their leisure in the weeks that followed. This Richard, intact save for the stripped down engine, has a conventional long range fuel tank under its starboard wing, but carries a primitive ground attack rocket launching pod under the port wing. *(James V. Crow)*

Above: An RAF officer views the cockpit of a totally demolished *Stuka* which carries desert camouflage, the code letters of St.G.1 and a white spinner nose. Either attempts have been made to cut out the diving raven emblem of II./St.G. 1 from the fuselage, or a total demolition job has been carried out which gives a good view of the composition of the Junker's 'double wing' form. The all-metal, two-spar construction panels (port and starboard) were attached to stub spars of the centre section on which the officer is standing. The plan form had a pronounced forward taper to the trailing edge. The duralumin ribs were riveted to the spars and the skin was of smooth duralumin sheeting, which was flush-riveted, with semi-protruding head rivets in a few places on the wing's underside. Four-section slotted flaps were attached to the extensions of the main ribs, five on each side, and the flaps and the mass-balanced ailerons protruded below and behind the wing. *(Ken Merrick)*

Above: A battle-weary Ju 87 of 237 *Squadriglia* undergoing repair and refitting on the Sicilian airfield of Giona del Colle in the summer of 1943. *(James V. Crow)*

Below: To help fight General Tito's Communist guerrillas in Yugoslavia many *Stuka* dive bombers were moved across the Adriatic and St.G. 51 was reformed to carry out anti-partisan operations. They bombed Vis Island where it was thought Tito was hiding, destroying *caiques* in the harbour and other installations and supported several full scale army sweeps into the mountains. This is an aircraft of the Stab. III./St.G. 51. *(Archiv Von Lutz)*

Below: A German Ju 87D stands on the edge of an Sicilian airfield in the summer heat of 1943 undergoing engine and other maintenance. In the face of the Allied threat the German *Stuka* force in the central Mediterranean, re-organised under *Luftflotte* 2 commanded by *Generalfeldmarschal* Wolfram *Freiherr* von Richthofen, was increased from seventy aircraft on 14 May 1943 to 150 by 3 July of the same year, but many of these were hived off to the Balkans, Greece and Sardinia. They thus took only a small part in operations against the Allied landings in Sicily and later at Salerno on the Italian mainland. *(Archiv Von Lutz)*

Opposite page, top: As the Allies slowly fought their way up the Italian mainland against stubborn German defence, they came across damaged and abandoned *Stuka*s on the various airfields they captured on the way. Here an American Lieutenant poses in front of the wreck of a Ju 87 belonging to the 9.III./SG. 3 (*Stukagruppen* were re-designated as *Schlachtgruppen* from October 1943) somewhere in Italy. *(Peter Snitzer via James V. Crow)*

Above: Another abandoned *Stuka*, this time the aircraft is an engineless Ju 87 of the Italian 206 *Squadriglia*, part of 121º *Gruppo* which was led by Captain Zucca up until the Italian Armistice in September, 1943. *(Peter J. Andrews via James V. Crow)*

Left: A view of another Italian Ju 87D of 237 *Squadriglia* with many problems, abandoned on Palermo airfield, Sicily in July 1943. The rear canopy is missing, the tips of the propeller are well chewed up, indicating a nose-up landing, the starboard undercarriage has collapsed and the wing is shored up by way of the underwing bomb carrier, while the engine was undergoing maintenance. This photograph is interesting in that it reveals details usually hidden from the camera, as, for example, the fuselage mounting of the aircraft's swinging bomb crutch, the port side engine coolant header tank and the armoured, seat-mounted pilot's headrest. *(Mrs Ellis via James V. Crow)*

Left: One of the last Italian dive bomber units to continue operations was 216 *Squadriglia*, of the 121° *Gruppo Autonomo Bombardamento a Tuffo*, seen here taxiing along the runway of Capua airport, Naples in August 1943. *(AMI via Nicola Malizia)*

Below left: When the Italians surrendered in September 1943, the Balkans, Greece and the island garrisons in the Aegean were left in limbo. Hitler determined to secure his southern flank and moved swiftly ordering in *Luftwaffe* units from as far afield as Russia. The St.G. 3 and the St.G. 51 operated over Corfu and then the former moved down to Rhodes. The Allies moved troops to occupy Leros, Cos and Samos, but without proper air cover. The *Stukas* once more resumed their dominance of the whole theatre of operations. Here the St.G. 3 delivers an attack on a British squadron on 8

October 1943 and the light cruiser HMS *Sirius* is near missed astern by a brace of heavy bombs. *(Jack Banner)*

Above: Some *Stuka* units, taken over by the 1943 Italian anti-fascist government that joined the Allies, continued to operate in a limited auxiliary role in Italy. Here an unarmed Dora is seen taking off from a badly damaged central Italian airfield. The aircraft is wearing the roundels of the *Aviazione Militare Italiana* (AMI) fighting on the Allied side. *(James V. Crow)*

Below: This photograph, taken from the British destroyer HMS *Faulknor*, shows a heavy *Stuka* attack by St.G. 3 on a British naval squadron as it leaves the Aegean after attacking a German troop convoy on 8th October 1943. *(Jack Banner)*

Above: Close-up of a Ju 87D-3 (WerkNr. 7580) of the AMI. The aircraft is seen here at Leece airport, south of Brindisi, in 1944. It is not operational, having no rear cockpit, and although it has new markings, the original *Luftwaffe* wheel spat individual aircraft letters are still retained. *(Andrew J. Pater via James V. Crow)*

Opposite page, top: The AMI was formed to replace the *Regia Aeronautica* and continued fighting on the Allied side. This is a Ju 87D-3 (WerkNr. 7579) of that force at Leece airport in 1944. *(Andrew J. Pater via James V. Crow)*

Right: A few intact German *Stuka*s were captured as the front line in Italy moved northwards again and one of these, a Ju 87D, is seen here at Leece airfield on the western Adriatic coast of the heel of Italy, with the new AMI markings on the fuselage, but the old German markings still very much in evidence via the swastika on the tail. In the background can be seen a P-39 Airacobra fighter. *(Amos Nicholson via James V. Crow)*

Right and below: Two further views of a captured German *Stuka* at Leece airfield with the new AMI markings on the fuselage, but the old German markings in evidence on the tail. *(James V. Crow)*

Opposite page, bottom: While the few Italian *Stuka*s that remained in the north fought for Mussolini with the *Aviazione Republicana*, those that remained in the south of the country fought with the Allies as the *Aviazione Militare Italiana.* Here a solitary Dora is seen between two Macchi MC 202 or 205 fighters in the late AMI markings outside hangars at Camp Galitino, Leece in 1944. *(Norman Becker via James V. Crow)*

Above: Normal *Stuka* operations continued unabated in the Balkans as guerrilla operations increased and the Soviet army menaced from the east as they overran Hungary and threatened Belgrade. Here a *Stuka* of the 7. *Staffel* of II./LLG. 1 is seen undergoing engine overhaul at the airfield of Rann, ten kilometres north of Agram, Croatia in June 1944. *(Helmut Mahr via James V. Crow)*

Left: By far the greatest contribution the Junkers Ju 87 made to the final defence of the Reich, in Italy as elsewhere, was through the night harassment operations of the specially converted *Stuka*s of the *Nachtschlachtgruppen* (NSG). These aircraft, the short-wing D-8 (ex-D-5) and the long-wing D-7 (specially modified D-3), were equipped with special night navigation equipment and extra radio apparatus, like the FuG 16z and the FuG 25, plus Direction Finding (D/F) loop aerials for the Egon target location system. To work in the darkness their engine exhausts were fitted with extensions that led over the wing root (seen clearly here, although incomplete) while their wing guns had flash shields fitted to them to reduce glare. *(James V. Crow)*

C. B. Macpherson
Dilemmas of Liberalism and Socialism

NEW WORLD PERSPECTIVES
General Editors   *Arthur and Marilouise Kroker*

Critical explorations of the key thinkers in the New World. Intersecting biography and history, individual monographs in *New World Perspectives* examine the central intellectual vision of leading contributors to politics, culture and society. *New World Perspectives* focus on decisive figures across the broad spectrum of contemporary discourse in art, literature and thought, each in the context of their relationship to the social movements of their times. Moving between the historically specific and the culturally universal, the series as a whole is intended to be both a celebration of the uniqueness of New World thought and a critical appraisal of its most dynamic tendencies, past and present.

AVAILABLE

TECHNOLOGY AND THE CANADIAN MIND: INNIS/McLUHAN/GRANT
Arthur Kroker

NORTHROP FRYE: A VISION OF THE NEW WORLD
David Cook

CULTURE CRITIQUE: FERNAND DUMONT AND NEW QUEBEC SOCIOLOGY
Michael A. Weinstein

C. B. Macpherson
Dilemmas of Liberalism and Socialism

William Leiss

St. Martin's Press
New York

First published in the United States of America in 1989

Printed and bounded in Canada

ISBN 0-312-02475-4

Library of Congress Cataloging-in-Publication Data

Leiss, William, 1939-
    C. B. Macpherson: dilemmas of liberalism and socialism/by
William Leiss.
      p. cm.
    Bibliography: p.
    ISBN 0-312-02475-4: $35.00 (est.)
    1. Macpherson, C.B. (Crawford Brough), 1911-87--Contributions in
political science. 2. Macpherson, C.B. (Crawford Brough), 1911-87
--Contributions in economics. I. Title
JC253.M34L45 1989
320.5--dc19   88-21141
                                                      CIP

To the memory of my teachers
Herbert Gutman, historian
Herbert Marcuse, philosopher

CONTENTS

Preface   9

1

Scope of the Work   11

2

Formation (1930-1955)
Preliminaries   20
Education and career   25
Trade unions and the state   30
Foundations (1936-1942)   45
Development (1943-1955)   57

3

Maturity (1955-1985)
The scholar as protagonist   74
Five themes   81
Economic sphere: the marketplace   85
  1. the institutional context   86
  2. the individual context   89
Economic sphere: individuals as doers
  and consumers   93
The capitalist agenda   101
Political sphere: property versus democracy   103
Conclusion: the liberal state   109

4

Canada as a Quasi-Market Society 112

Legacy 113
The nature of a quasi-market society 115
When did the transition from capitalism
  to socialism occur? 119
OECD nations as quasi-market societies 124
  1. society: public sector economic
    activity 125
  2. society: business regulation and
    subsidies 127
  3. capital concentration 128
  4. individuals: income distribution 130
  5. transfer payments and the welfare
    floor 132
Three issues 134

5

Epilogue: An Appreciation 143

Notes 147

References 150

Preface

Just as a biographer must allow his own life history to pass before his eyes while detailing his subject's story, so too the author of an intellectual biography cannot help but conduct a self-examination while pursuing his topic. The treatment of Brough Macpherson's university education in this volume brought back warm memories of my own apprenticeship with gifted and generous teachers. The upwelling of these recollections was a delightful and wholly unexpected benefit that accrued to me during the writing of this book, and I am deeply grateful for it.

I was invited to write this contribution for the New World Perspectives series some years ago by Arthur and Marilouise Kroker. Although the Krokers are responsible for its genesis, the project could not have been completed without the expert assistance of Richard Smith, a doctoral student in the Department of Communication at Simon Fraser University. Richard assembled the bibliographical resources and tracked down much of the secondary literature, and organized it all superbly. In addition, discussions with him helped to structure the book and finally, his assistance with wordprocessing and electronic communication systems was (and continues to be) indispensable. It is a pleasure to be associated with him.

Every commentator on Macpherson's work is indebted to Victor Svacek for his comprehensive Macpherson bibliography, published in *Powers, Possessions and Freedom: Essays in Honour of C. B. Macpherson*, edited by Alkis Kontos (University of Toronto Press, 1979). I would like to thank Alkis Kontos for his invitation to me to contribute to that volume and the University of Toronto Press for permitting me to use some portions of my contribution, "Marx and Macpherson: Needs, Utilities and Self-Development," in this volume.

Some years ago three anonymous evaluators warmly recommended this project for assistance to the Social Sciences and Humanities Research Council of Canada, and the SSHRCC very kindly provided the two grants that were requested. Three readers of the first draft made suggestions for revisions, some of which have been incorporated into the finished text. Most helpful of all was the additional detailed commentary done at my request by my friend and colleague at Simon Fraser, Professor Heribert Adam.

The collegial and intensely productive atmosphere in the Department of Communication at Simon Fraser University provides a great stimulus for scholarly research and writing, and it is my good fortune to partake of it.

Only Marilyn Lawrence has shared all of my book projects, and I am very glad that she is willing to entertain still more. And finally, I am thankful that Brough Macpherson took the time to discuss with me his early education and career during a long and pleasant conversation at his home in the Summer of 1986.

Vancouver, B. C.

1

Scope of the Work

All political theorists are utopians, more or less. Few among Plato's successors could resist being seduced by his bold scheme, but some were more willing than others to display their infatuation. Thus there have been two basic forms of utopianism over the centuries, one in which a plan for a better world was proclaimed aloud and another, more reticent but not necessarily less committed, in which discreet allusions to the need for changing the world were embedded in the critique of existing conditions.

C. B. Macpherson was a political theorist of the latter sort. With extraordinary consistency and tenacity throughout a teaching and writing career spanning more than four decades, he anchored his study of politics in a claim that a better society was possible. Although the nature of the claim was clear enough it was never developed into a full-fledged argument, nor did its advocacy go beyond the gentle remonstrances of the printed page and the public address. Certainly his critical stance had enough in common with Marxism to make it easy for some to place him in that camp; however, the methodically undogmatic character of his thought, together with an aversion to invocations of specific remedies, clearly made him uncomfortable with the notion of wearing ideological labels.

All told his writings are marked clearly from the very first with a utopian intent, yet another feature is equally evident, namely a firm detachment from orthodoxies and an independence of purpose. As I see it, both arose simultaneously out of his choosing political theory as a lifelong vocation during his undergraduate years. He was not publicly a notable activist in domains outside those of his academic profession; by his own account, in the domestic division of labor agreed upon with his wife Kay, he would remain the theorist. Moreover, from the outset Macpherson appeared to be content to express his views largely within the compass of the academic world, and in doing so he crafted a prose style marked by a directness and elegant simplicity that is rarely seen in academic discourse.

To take up the serious pursuit of political theory's ancient concerns in a university setting demanded adherence to the accepted canons of scholarly debate, and Macpherson never wavered in his allegiance to them. He was most fortunate in finding a faculty position in political theory at his alma mater just when he had completed his postgraduate studies in England — although the year was 1935, not the most propitious of times; certainly this uninterrupted attachment to a university setting helped to cement his allegiance to it. The Canadian university system repaid that allegiance by bestowing unhindered career progress and, later, some of its highest honors on this unrepentant critic of contemporary institutions.

The major purpose of this short study is to suggest that Macpherson's thought can be understood best as the outcome of his distinctive mode of practicing political theory as a vocation. Essentially, his practice consisted of an examination of the origins and development of modern political issues, an examination which has, at one and the

same time and without internal inconsistency, a commitment to both scholarly forms of debate and to the cause
of social improvement. A look at his earliest published
writings shows that this double-sided commitment was
already fully formed then, and thus that it can be considered to be a product of his university education. It became a lasting part of his career.

In his commitment to the cause of social improvement
Macpherson fits the description of the "epic theorist" given
by Sheldon Wolin in his essay, "Political Theory as a Vocation." The epic theorist "seeks to reassemble the whole
political world," including a reorientation of accepted ways
of imagining and accounting for what we do (as well as
what we ought to do) in everyday social life. The work
of an epic theorist is also marked by the "quality of car-
ing for public things (*res publicae*)," that is, an explicit
commitment to promoting the common good. Finally, and
as a derivative of these two features, the epic theorist, who
entertains the possibility that the existing political order
is systematically flawed, constructs a political theory which
"takes the form of a symbolic picture of an ordered whole,"
that is, a vision of a better world which does not take the
present-day "facts" of existence as an eternal condition
of humanity.[1]

Macpherson's contributions as an epic theorist are expressed primarily in his lifelong preoccupation with the
successes and failures of liberal political thought, as well
as liberal political practice in the history of the modern
state. His studies of English liberalism emphasized its severe limitations (as well as its accomplishments) as a basis
for a fully acceptable theory and practice of democracy.
For Macpherson liberalism had capitulated at its origins
to the overriding requirements of "bourgeois society," and
this subordination would have to be reversed sooner or
later. Yet he insisted that liberalism's achievements, no matter how defective, were an indispensable starting-point for
further social progress; for example, an essay published
in 1985 states that without civil liberties, democracy is a
"travesty."[2] Among the thinkers of his generation who

shared some form of the "radical" critique of capitalism, Macpherson stands out as perhaps the most important native North American theorist, and a good deal of his importance lies in his consistent defense of liberal political values as an essential part of this critique.

In my view this defense is a logical outcome of the other side of his dual commitment, that is, his commitment to scholarly pursuits. For the honest practice of the scholar's trade demands explicit adherence to liberal values: freedom of expression, canons of fairness in argument, equality of opportunity for participation, protection against persecution for opinions, tolerance, and the search for truth. These, however, were never intended by their originators to be reserved exclusively for the scholar's enclaves, and a demand to institute them as fully as possible everywhere in society flows from their very nature; the theorist's task is to name and expose the obstacles to their realization. In other words, to start not from a commitment to scholarship alone but rather from its combination with the cause of social improvement meant that one had to take the essential values of liberalism very seriously indeed. This compelled one to explain why liberalism had failed to realize its potentialities as a progressive force in society and to assist in a renewed endeavor to actualize those potentialities.

There was no unanimity on this point. Among Macpherson's contemporaries many championed the cause of social improvement — among Marxists and others of the Left, and among the Right (which has its own version of improvements) as well — while scorning liberalism and all its works. Little surprise is occasioned when this view is proclaimed and practiced by the Right. Alas, too little surprise occurred among some adherents of the Left in similar circumstances, when charlatans proposed that the masses must be led to their salvation by fair means or foul. Macpherson's double-sided commitment ruled out this course and required that liberalism, shorn of its inconsistencies and false presuppositions, be a partner in prosecuting that cause. Holding this view set a specific agenda for a theorist — namely, to expose the ties between liberalism and capitalism and to propose undoing them.

Among the prominent twentieth-century critics of capitalism in North American and Western Europe only one other group of thinkers shared Macpherson's long preoccupation with liberalism: the Frankfurt School, especially Herbert Marcuse and Max Horkheimer. Both Marcuse and Horkheimer wrote bold interpretive essays on liberalism in the nineteen-thirties, and Marcuse returned to these themes much later in "Repressive Tolerance" (1965) and *An Essay on Liberation* (1969).[3] Marcuse left an ambiguous bequest to the liberal legacy: he appeared to abandon liberalism in those published works of the nineteen-sixties while continuing to reaffirm it "in private," that is, in his practice of intellectual work. On the other hand, Macpherson never publicly attacked liberal values and thus he occupies a distinctive place in this influential current of thought.

His treatment of liberalism was not merely a philosophical exercise. From the very beginning of his career, Macpherson had situated it within a theory of social institutions. This theory is grounded in the concept of property, the discussion of which is the single most consistent theme in his life's work spanning half a century: "property" is the main consideration in his master's thesis, presented at the London School of Economics in 1935, and it is still featured in two of the essays in the collection published in 1985 entitled *The Rise and Fall of Economic Justice*. The tension between the heritage of liberalism and the values of individual freedom that it brings to the conduct of politics, on the one hand, and the deeply-rooted inequalities in the institutional order which are shielded by the structure of property ownership, on the other, forms the underlying unity of Macpherson's thought. His theory of social change, which is based on the concept of "developmental powers," represents his attempt to resolve this tension in a way that is consistent with the tradition of epic theory.

The manner in which he works this out constitutes his "method" as an epic theorist. He begins by presenting an opposition between a pair of mutually exclusive "models" of behavior, patterns of thinking, or paths of social development. Then the claim is made that the choice of one model, pattern, or path will result over time in resolving the tension previously described. A number of instances in which Macpherson used this method effectively will be mentioned in the chapters that follow.

The commentary on Macpherson's writings offered in this essay will be guided by the interpretive scheme outlined above. In other words, I will set out the nature of his double-sided commitment and trace its impact on the intellectual content of his output. The task of exposition is made simple by virtue of Macpherson's extraordinary consistency: the guiding perspective in his work is notable for its fixity rather than for its evolution. Macpherson gripped the image of society he wished to undermine with remarkable tenacity; having affixed that grip early in life and refusing to change it thereafter, he remained very close to his original conception of his antagonist, with the result that his critique misses the implications of some major social transformations that occurred during his lifetime.

Yet one must also admit that a portrait of society composed of images of mutually exclusive choices is not meant to be "read" literally. Rather, the point is to forcefully draw the reader's attention to what is claimed to be the essential features in the picture as a whole (for Macpherson the essential feature is the role of the marketplace in modern society), and to do so repeatedly, if need be, so as to overcome the natural tendency of readers and audiences to become distracted and inattentive. Once accomplished, the patterns in events can be seen more clearly. I count myself among those who have benefited from encountering his work.

Like his guiding perspective Macpherson's life and career is also notable for its fixity: forty-five years of uninterrupted university appointment in the same department at a university located in the city where he was born, with only one brief leave taken in a nonacademic setting! The commitment to scholarly pursuits and liberal values that sustained this career shows itself in both the form and content of his published writings. Rarely was an opportunity to engage in debate missed, it must be noted, as a long series of replies to critics attests. Another indicator is the extraordinary string of book reviews he wrote in a wide variety of journals: beginning in 1936 and continuing almost uninterrupted thereafter hardly a year elapsed without such a review being published. The titles of the books he reviewed are about evenly distributed between "mainstream" and "critical" works, mostly of the academic sort, and the reviews provide some interesting clues to Macpherson's interests and outlook, especially since the citation of secondary literature in his own books and articles tends to be rather sparse.

This book begins with a detailed look at the period which runs from his undergraduate days at the University of Toronto (1929-1932) to 1955. I take a close look at his master's thesis, a 325-page opus presented in 1935. The phase extending from 1936 to 1942 contains the solid basis for the interpretive scheme I wish to defend, namely that the core of Macpherson's contribution lies in his dual commitment to social improvement and scholarly pursuits, as unified in the notion of political theory as a vocation.

The next phase in my scheme includes 1943 to 1955 and encompasses *Democracy in Alberta* (1953) and the first mention (in a 1954 essay entitled "The Deceptive Task of Political Theory") of the phrase "possessive individualism." The events during this period are significant. In the nineteen-forties Macpherson had set out a major role for political theory within the discipline of political science: theory was to serve as a "principle of unity" for the discipline as a whole and was to do so by concentrating on "the interaction of political ideas and concrete political facts." Nevertheless, the analysis presented in *Democracy in Alberta*, with its attempted integration of institutional and theoretical analysis, did not fulfill the mission for political theory that had been articulated by Macpherson himself.

In fact his grand project for theory was largely abandoned thereafter. Instead, understanding liberalism's ambiguous heritage through the concept of possessive individualism, together with a major elaboration of the critique of capitalist society that is based on this concept, occupied most of Macpherson's time and effort without interruption from 1955 and thirty years onwards.

I do not intend to recapitulate Macpherson's understanding of liberal thought — except insofar as it bears on his critique of capitalism — or the academic controversies touched off by it. Certainly I do not mean thereby to belittle his significant contribution to scholarly debates on political theory in the past quarter-century: The number of conference papers and published articles and special conference sessions devoted to his work testify amply to the scope and challenge of Macpherson's spirited forays into this domain. Nevertheless, such debates, however learned and influential they may be, are the conventional stuff of academic life, clouds of interpretation perpetually swirling over the intellectual landscape: Some formations are more interesting than others in the same sky, and all will be succeeded in turn by fresher ones in the new day.

To my mind that which is truly distinctive about Macpherson's thought and career is not the battles over Hobbes, Locke and the rest, but rather his steadfast adherence to the double-sided commitment outlined above, or to what I have called his practice of political theory as a vocation. A biographical treatment might attempt to fill out this portrait with documents and anecdotes drawn from his university career, interviews with former colleagues and students, and passages from his correspondence; for the present project, however, I have had to confine myself primarily to published writings. The important materials for this project, then, are first the subsidiary comments in book reviews, articles, and books which reveal Macpherson's personal and intellectual stance, and second the theoretical apparatus that he crafted for the critique of capitalism and the imagining of a better society.

Thus the focus of the interpretation offered in the following pages may be summarized as follows. Macpherson's practice of political theory as a vocation has two interconnected dimensions. One is his commitment to the scholar's craft, which considered in terms of its social context leads to his lifelong defense of liberal political values. The other is his commitment to social justice, and it leads to his conception of modern society as founded upon what appears to be a permanent state of tension between political freedom and property rights. Macpherson's method is to seek to break free of this underlying tension or dilemma by posing a series of choices between mutually exclusive options for future social development (which are in turn based upon mutually exclusive ways of seeing the social world), and by suggesting that choosing one option over another will enable us to overcome the dilemma and to achieve both freedom and justice. Finally, it is suggested that we are not meant to take literally this posing of options, but rather to make use of the clarification it brings in order to identify the essential features of actual political and social choices now.

2

Formation: 1930 to 1955

Preliminaries

Crawford Brough Macpherson's life spanned a period of extraordinary social change. He began his university training within months of the stock-market debacle in 1929 and finished that training while the Great Depression persisted. He took up professional writing at a time when the still vibrant ideological currents inherited from the nineteenth century — capitalism versus socialism and communism — had been amplified by the special circumstances of the day: the long economic crisis of capitalist nations, the sporadic militancy of working-class organizations, the rise of European fascism, and the hopes and illusions bound with the fate of the Soviet Union. He was fortunate to be able to embark upon his chosen career immediately upon completion of his graduate studies, and gradually he attained national and international prominence in academic circles during that unusual period in the quarter-century after 1945 when Western capitalism attained a level of general economic prosperity that most social commentators writing in the 1930s could not have imagined to be possible.

His first publications were a few short book reviews in a left-wing journal dedicated to influencing social change. This was only a brief foray, however, and within a few years he had begun to publish almost exclusively in academic and semi-academic journals; thereafter he never wrote more that an occasional short piece in any other venue. In no sense did he "trim" his outlook to fit an academic mold. Rather, it seems clear that he set for himself the mission of winning recognition for his viewpoint within the Canadian university system and having it accepted there permanently as a legitimate contender in academic debates. In this he succeeded brilliantly: there can be little doubt that in the postwar period Macpherson was one of a small group of influential thinkers in the English-speaking world who widened the boundaries of academic discourse in the social sciences, by requiring the keepers of the then-prevailing orthodoxies to admit into the fold what we might loosely call a "socialist" perspective.

For a short period during the Second World War he took a leave from his university position to work at a minor government task, but this was the only interruption in an academic career that spanned forty-five years. During the war he also published his first strictly academic piece of scholarship, and by 1945 he was fully committed to producing the stream of essays and books that eventually would bring him worldwide recognition as a scholar. Both the interpretive slant of his scholarly contributions, and the explicit concerns of the essays he devoted to contemporary social issues put him unmistakably on the "left" side of the ideological spectrum throughout his career.

Certainly Macpherson can be regarded as a "socialist" thinker, although such appellations should be used with caution, since he refused to apply them publicly to himself. What is undeniable is his lifelong interest in the advancement of a set of goals for social change that are usually identified with the cause of democratic socialism. This commitment, forged early in his intellectual development, was unaffected by the progress of his academic career. It was also unaffected by the social changes occurring in Western societies in the period after 1945 — and this fact prompts me to undertake at the end of this book some retouching of the picture he painted of contemporary society and its problems.

Western societies (the nations of North America and Western Europe) moved from what was still (in 1930) primarily a laissez-faire political economy in the late-nineteenth-century mold to what now has been called by Macpherson and others "managed capitalism" or a "mixed economy." Yet where ideological debates about social change persist (always more so in Europe than in North America), the enormous changes in political economy are often poorly reflected in those debates. Much ideological struggle still revolves majestically around the classical nineteenth-century polarization between capitalism and socialism, with the participants in this struggle seemingly unaware that a qualitatively different social order — representing a kind of compromise or convergence of the two older models — has taken root. Furthermore this is true not only of the somewhat esoteric debates conducted in academic circles and among the adherents of various sects: whenever strong polarization occurs in political life in the West (such as happens often in Great Britain or British Columbia, for example), the same representations emerge and the public is confronted by the allegedly momentous choice between "free enterprise" and "socialism."

In other words, a good deal of ideological debate about politics and society has lagged behind actual social development during the past half-century and indeed has not yet succeeded in coming to terms with it. Some insight into this situation and the reasons for its persistence can be found in Macpherson's writings. Like other thinkers before him, Macpherson sought to understand the peculiar dynamic of capitalism, a form of political economy that embodied for so long such an enormous disparity between the social benefits — primarily genuine democracy and economic well-being — it promised on the one hand, and the insufficient measure of those benefits actually delivered to date on the other. Macpherson believed that capitalism's foundations remained intact up to the present day and also that this system was inherently incapable of delivering that genuine democracy and well-being. Therefore, the terms in which he presented his pairs of mutually exclusive options for future social change essentially stayed bound to the classical ideological polarization between capitalism and socialism.

Certainly, the basic analytical categories fashioned for the socialist critique of capitalism in the nineteenth century (the property system, social classes, wage labor, the commodity form) remain serviceable, since many basic features in the institutional structures of a capitalist form of political economy persist. In a dynamic social system such as modern capitalism, however, the "object of analysis" for the commentator — that is, the form of political economy — does not sit still for the operation. Rather it mutates whilst being observed, thus challenging analysts to retool their conceptual armory regularly. Marx himself, who had described capitalism as a "permanently revolutionary" social form, failed to see the full impact of this observation on his own concepts. Macpherson too did not see with sufficient clarity that capitalism, although it is like many others a class-based form of political economy, has a peculiarly dynamic character that distinguishes it from its relatively more static predecessors. This feature sets a basic requirement for those who seek to analyze its "laws of movement," namely to trace its continuous institutional transformations in detail and to ensure that the concepts designed to grasp those laws are regularly refined. I will try to show that Macpherson's key pairs of options, although they were always presented in an elegant and incisive fashion, failed in part the test of this requirement.

In my treatment of Macpherson as a political theorist of the "epic" sort — that is, as one who in Wolin's terms cares for public things and draws a picture of an ordered whole — I will focus on this point, namely the relation between his key categories and the society they comprehend. For example, I will track what he has to say about "property" from his first extensive use of it in his 1935 master's thesis to his last publications. I will ask what his use of this term is intended to "do" and to what extent the effort succeeds. This type of judgement is appropriate for the work of epic theorists, who set for themselves the pragmatic objective of reorienting the accepted ways of imagining both what we do and what we ought to do in politics and society.

The concept of property in which his theory of social institutions is embodied is one of the three central and interrelated themes in Macpherson's writings that will be followed in this book. The second is democracy or the theory of politics, including such institutionalized forms as the party system. As mentioned earlier, I will not comment directly on the scholarly controversies triggered by Macpherson's interpretation of the history of liberal political theory; rather, my discussion of democracy will focus on the relation between political systems and social institutions. The third theme is the individual, or more precisely the connection between individuals and society. The best illustration of this theme is the contrast between "developmental" and "acquisitive" powers; and in general this is the utopian element in Macpherson's thought, the one which shows most clearly his acceptance of political theory as a vocation.

Macpherson was a perceptive and forceful critic of contemporary society, as well as a writer whose masterful prose style earned him a permanent place in the tradition of epic theory in politics. It should be obvious that his high standing in this regard is not diminished by any discussion that deals with the weaknesses, in addition to the strengths, to be found in his outlook. For in theoretical matters just as in material life, the successes of preceding generations become their bequest to us and require nothing save suitable appreciation on our part; more valuable are their artful deficiencies, since we can exercise and develop our own powers in striving to ferret out and overcome them.

Education and Career

C. B. Macpherson entered the University of Toronto for undergraduate studies in 1929 at the age of eighteen and was graduated in 1932.[1] He began to read modern political theory at this time but took no other formal training in the history of political thought, apart from attending some lectures on Plato by a philosopher, Fulton Anderson. He also studied the economic theory of Marshall and others with Professor E. J. Urwick, who had retired from the London School of Economics before going to Toronto; Macpherson later taught this subject for a number of years during the early part of his academic career. It was during his undergraduate days that Macpherson made a firm choice about pursuing academic life as a career.

At this point he also had decided upon political theory as his chief intellectual interest and academic specialization. Almost certainly this was the result of the teacher who had influenced him most as an undergraduate, Otto B. van der Sprenkel, who must have been someone quite different from most other professors at the University of Toronto then. Van der Sprenkel was one of the growing number of left-wing intellectuals who were fleeing the European continent in the early 1930s before the rising tide of fascism; he had first gone to England and had been a student of Harold Laski's at the London School of Economics. He then secured a post as a lecturer in the University of Toronto's Department of Political Economy for two years, before leaving Canada and settling in Australia, whereupon he became a Sinologist, because (as Macpherson recalls him saying) he found political theory "too easy."

I have not been able to find much trace of van der

Sprenkel's outlook and work, but a few notes on them may be of interest, since Macpherson remembered his teaching as a major factor in forming his own orientation as a young scholar. Van der Sprenkel published a short piece in the *Canadian Forum* in June 1932 entitled "The Fantasies of Mr. Havelock" in which he stated: "We are living in a time when, on the one hand, there is a vast movement of dissatisfaction among the masses, on the other hand, hysterical fear and a growing lack of self confidence amongst those who live by owning, and who direct commerce and industry." He concluded with what appears to be an oblique defense of the Communist Party. He resurfaced again as one of three authors of a book entitled *New China: Three Views*, published in 1951. A reviewer in the journal *Pacific Affairs* noted that all three authors had had first-hand experience of China after 1949; according to him, van der Sprenkel's chapter argues that China will be able to achieve economic development without foreign aid, and moreover that China will pursue an independent course in relation to the Soviet Union. These views are also aired in a series of short essays which van der Sprenkel wrote for the *Spectator* in 1955, which show a solid acquaintance with past history and current events in China.[2]

Macpherson was introduced to modern political thought by van der Sprenkel. He read some work by Marx for the first time then — volume I of *Capital* and parts of what would later become known as *The Economic and Philosophical Manuscripts of 1844* (which Macpherson had in an English translation reproduced in mimeo by a Trotskyist group in New York). Macpherson recalled during our conversation in 1986 that he had found *Capital* "rather confused" and that Marx's work as a whole was never a major influence on his own thinking. Van der Sprenkel's frequent references to Laski, however, together with a first reading of some of Laski's books, convinced Macpherson that he should try to do graduate study with Laski at the London School of Economics; he was accepted and moved to London in 1932.

Harold Joseph Laski (1893-1950), a native of Manchester, was a prolific writer of both academic and semi-popular treatises, a major figure in the development of the Labour Party (as well as the Fabian Society) — he was the Labour Party's chairman in 1945 when it formed a government in Britain for the first time — and a well-known public speaker, as well as an influential university teacher. He taught briefly at McGill University in 1915, then at Harvard, before returning to Britain and taking up a post at the London School of Economics in 1920, where he remained on the staff until his death. He authored upwards of thirty books (including the remarkable published correspondence with the American jurist Oliver Wendell Holmes, Jr.) and hundreds of articles and pamphlets. By the 1920s Laski was firmly committed to democratic socialism of a non-dogmatic sort and to its achievement by peaceful means. But as the economic crisis deepened throughout the 1920s and 1930s, and as the rise of fascism began to threaten the social progress achieved up to then, he became convinced that some degree of violence would inevitably accompany the transition from capitalism to socialism; only the end of the war and the electoral victory of the Labour Party modified this stance.[3]

Macpherson attended Laski's lectures on sixteenth-century French political theory and developed a broad interest in the history of ideas, including the history of European social thought, under his influence. He and other graduate students frequently were invited to tea at Laski's home, which had become a kind of way-station for European intellectuals in flight from fascism. There he met the other two members of a small "circle" comprised of Laski, R. H. Tawney, and the sociologist Morris Ginsberg.

Richard Henry Tawney (1880-1962) also exerted a strong influence on the young Macpherson. Tawney was an economic historian and social reformer whose first book, *The Agrarian Problem in the Sixteenth Century* (1912), made him famous. After teaching for many years in workers' education forums and advocating Christian Socialism in speeches and writings, he became a professor at the London School of Economics in 1931. His two best-known books were published in the 1920s: *The Acquisitive Society* (1920) and *Religion and the Rise of Capitalism* (1926). The former, which he had first published as a Fabian Society pamphlet under the title "The Sickness of an Acquisitive Society," is a powerful tract, its critique of capitalism and market relations grounded in an ethical position that was drawn from the elements of social radicalism in Christianity. Macpherson remarked in his 1986 conversation with me that his concept of "possessive individualism" was developed out of his search for a more precise expression for Tawney's notion of acquisitiveness.

Macpherson completed his graduate studies in April 1935 at the London School of Economics with a master's thesis, prepared under Laski's supervision, entitled "Voluntary Associations within the State, 1900-1934, with special reference to the Place of Trade Unions in relation to the State in Great Britain." In that same year Macpherson sought a teaching position and wrote to Urwick, who was then Chair of the Department of Political Economy at the University of Toronto, and it was his great good fortune to find, amidst those terrible economic times, an opening in the field of political theory! He was appointed as a lecturer in political theory, beginning an uninterrupted association with the University of Toronto that would last until his retirement about forty-five years later.

He took a leave of absence from the University for thirty months in the years 1941 to 1943, first on a secondment to the Wartime Information Board in Ottawa. The Board was headed by John Grierson, and Macpherson's job was to review and write reports on the coverage by the Canadian press of the federal government's conduct and policies. The task included both the established English- and French-language newspapers and a collection of papers from what conventionally is called the "ethnic press," that is, small-circulation newspapers published in languages other than English or French. Macpherson had other officials doing the translations of articles from the latter for him. In his own words, his work as a wartime bureaucrat was "totally uneventful."

He then went to the University of New Brunswick for one academic year, in response to a request from someone he had met at the Wartime Information Board, to replace a professor who had left on short notice; he served there (in his own terms) as "professor of everything," teaching courses on introduction to economics, labor economics, British government, and comparative government. He returned to the University of Toronto in 1943. By that time he was married to Kay, who was already campaigning (as she would do throughout the 1940s) in federal and provincial ridings as a women's candidate for the Co-operative Commonwealth Federation. According to Macpherson they practiced a "domestic division of labor" between theory and practice for the entirety of their careers and lives together.[4]

When he returned to the University of Toronto Macpherson remained a lecturer for about six years before being promoted to the rank of assistant professor. No tenured or permanent appointment was granted in those days until promotion to associate professor was made, and normally this was dependent upon the publication of a book (in his case *Democracy in Alberta*, 1953). Harold Innis was his department chair by this time and Macpherson often joined him, the political economist V. W. Bladen, and the sociologist S.D. Clark at an informal "lunch table group" at the Faculty Club. Macpherson had attended a few of Innis's lectures on economic history as an undergraduate but had found them rather tedious: "He went on and on about the bloody fur traders," he remarked during our conversation in 1986.

While Macpherson was still an untenured assistant professor in the early 1950s, McCarthyism was taking its toll among universities and the professoriate in the United States. Macpherson could later recall no spillover into Canadian university life, however, and according to his own testimony he never experienced any detrimental effect resulting from the "socialist" orientation of his work during his entire career. He remembered only one minor episode in the early 1950s in which Innis told him that he [Innis] had had to listen to some offhand "complaint" about Macpherson's presumed political stance — but the matter went no further than that.

A final note on style. All readers of Macpherson's works can appreciate the limpid and jargon-free prose that makes them such a pleasure to read. Macpherson said that he had resolved from the beginning to write with clarity of expression and uncomplicated grammatical structure and that his model was Voltaire. His choice of this literary model says a great deal about what he hoped to accomplish by a lifetime of effort within a university's walls.

Trade Unions and the State: The Master's Thesis

I have devoted a special section to Macpherson's M.A. thesis for a number of reasons. First, it is the only substantial piece of his life's work that is generally unknown. Second, Macpherson embarked on his career at a time when Ph.D. programs in the social sciences were uncommon in the British system, so that he did no doctoral program and Ph.D. thesis. Instead, he took the normal route of submitting a collection of published papers (sixteen in all) some twenty years after completing his graduate work, and was awarded the DSc(Econ) degree by the London School of Economics in 1955. Third, it is a substantial work, with 322 pages of text, and he did not use the material later in his publications. Finally, in the subject-matter I find a weird resonance with local current events: as I write, the trade unions and the government of British Columbia are caught up in the latest of their regular province-wide confrontations, including the announcement of a "general strike."

Most of Macpherson's thesis is focussed on the theory and practice of the trade union movement in England in relation to the legal structure imposed on it by the state through legislation and judicial decisions. In their origins trade unions are of course "voluntary associations," like churches and religious movements, businesses, sports and other clubs, political parties, charitable agencies, and associations of professionals such as doctors and lawyers. Some of these eventually receive legal recognition by governments which then impose certain requirements on them, but many others continue as unincorporated bodies; trade unions attained legal standing in Britain upon the passage of the Trade Union Act, 1876. Macpherson adds a briefer discussion of another type of legally-recognized voluntary association (the British Medical Association) at the end, to provide some contrasting elements for his argument.

His emphasis on the workings of the state reflects the influence of his teacher, Harold Laski, who had written a long series of well-known books on the concepts of sovereignty and the state, concentrating on the history of the development of these doctrines since the sixteenth century, including a general work called *The State in Theory and Practice* (1935). Macpherson's list of references in his thesis includes, in addition to the directly relevant academic literature, a number of contemporary tracts, such as Tawney's "The Choice before the Labour Party" (1933), a Socialist League pamphlet, and Franz Neumann's "Trade Unionism, Democracy, Dictatorship" (1934), a Workers' Educational Trade Union Committee pamphlet. The theme of the relation between voluntary associations and the state, however, had been raised somewhat earlier in the academic literature on legal and political theory by two eminent British scholars, J. N. Figgis and F. W. Maitland, whose views are mentioned briefly.

Macpherson's approach to the relation between trade unions and the state in Britain is to look at the main points in the most important pieces of legislation and the key judicial decisions after 1871. The aim of the thesis is stated clearly; it is to show

> that both the general tendency of the law and
> its variation at different times are intelligible only
> on the assumption that in regulating the pow-

ers and status of trade unions the State has acted consistently on only one principle.

This principle is found to be the maintenance
of the essential basis of the existing industrial
system, that is, the structure of property relations
in it and, more broadly, the preservation of the
social institutions which serve to maintain those
property relations throughout the society.[5]

The key terms are used quite consistently throughout the
thesis: social institutions and the social system, the economic or industrial system, and the patterns of ownership
are all said to be based on the "system [or structure] of
property relations."

By the time we reach the end of the work the connections between the key terms are clear. The state is the
agent for dominant social interests which are determined
by the pattern of property relations; therefore, in its actions the state will be motivated by one overriding objective, namely the "protection" of existing property relations.
It is also clear that in his thesis Macpherson does not intend to put the propositions comprising the preceding sentence "to the test" of an argument, either theoretical or
empirical in nature. Rather, they will serve together as the
presupposition or postulate for his examination of trade
unions and the state. Moreover, his examination does not
and cannot demonstrate in any acceptable fashion that the
state has acted on *"only one* principle" (my italics), since
he does not survey a range of possible candidates and then
give reasons why the one singled out, that is the preservation of existing property relations, is the most deserving.

There is a straightforward explanation for these omis-
sions: Macpherson's exposition is dominated by a pragmatic objective, namely, the attempt to ascertain, on the
basis of his historical investigation, where the unions will
stand on the political choices to be made in the next phase
of the perilous times during which he wrote. This was stated in his opening pages: "[I will] consider the probable
future development of trade unions both in the capitalist

State and in the socialist State at which the unions are aiming."[6] As we shall see, the "choice" of either capitalism or socialism frames the entirety of Macpherson's exposition in his thesis; and of course it was something he shared with many European leftist intellectuals at that time, for whom the coming of fascism simply made urgent and inescapable the long-sought deliverance from capitalism through the mass-based socialist movements (for a small minority, through the Communist Party).

In developing his central theme, Macpherson focussed on what he called the "anomalous" position of the unions resulting from the application to them of laws and judicial decisions since 1871, the upshot of which was to leave the unions in a nether world somewhere between unincorporated voluntary associations and corporations. Before 1871, when only the common law was applicable, most unions and their activities were illegal *pro forma*, as combinations in restraint of trade, for under the common law freedom of trade was interpreted as the unfettered operation of labor markets between the buyers and sellers of labor power. The Trade Union Act of 1871 exempted unions from these strictures of the common law when they were pursuing certain recognized (statutory) objectives, for example striking for better wages. Unions attained legal recognition as voluntary associations, which also allowed them to hold property and administer trust funds; the Act of 1913 formalized this procedure by granting the Registrar of Friendly Societies the authority to register or certify a trade union for the purposes of the Act. There was, however, no legal compulsion to be registered or certified; those unions that were not so registered continued to be treated under the law as unincorporated voluntary associations, and in fact the legal privileges pertaining to registered status were quite minor.

In the forty years after 1871, however, union membership and the economic power of unions grew rapidly, and in the period before World War I the government was forced to recognize for the first time the political power of the union movement and the Labour Party. During the parliamentary debates on the Trades Disputes Act (1906), Macpherson observes, the "Opposition as well as the Government agreed that trade unions were now an indispensable part of the industrial system and were a force for order and peace in industry."[7] The main reason for this revelation was that the unions had begun to show that they could provide an institutional mechanism for reaching agreements on wages and working conditions and for controlling the outbreak of strikes and walkouts.

The Act of 1913 addressed a number of specific issues, especially the formulation of rules for the collection and use by unions of their members' dues for political causes. More important, however, was the official recognition of the principles behind the Act of 1906, namely that in the "negotiation" among social interests the working class (represented by the trade union movement) would be included as an acknowledged member. The parliamentary debates at the time reveal, in Macpherson's words, "the conviction shared by all parties that the trade unions were not only a necessary and accepted part of the industrial structure but also a valuable stabilizing element among workers." He gives a splendid extract from a speech by the Attorney-General of the moment on this point:

> I do not think anyone who knows anything of the conditions of labour in this country will dispute that in trade unions you will find your best class of working men, and the more support and strength you give to the bodies which unite those men, the better it is for the stability of the industries of this country.[8]

In effect, a new "social contract" was being fashioned.

Thus another social interest had been identified, a "third term," as it were, to stand between the two permanently warring parties of capital and labor: the public interest. Promoting the idea of a public interest to achieve the basis for a certain orderliness in industrial relations attained some prominence in the 1906 parliamentary debates on the Trade Disputes Act, where it was mooted that (in view of labor's growing economic and political power) a condition of permanent and unrestrained antagonism between capitalists and workers would likely destroy much of the social and economic progress made in Britain to date. In 1906 it was not plainly stated that the solution to this dilemma would be to have the government act as an arbiter in this matter — that would come later; but the seeds of such an idea had been planted. Macpherson interprets this development as just another instance of "the State" acting "out of consideration for the interests of those who controlled the industrial structure."[9]

At this point Macpherson's routine, vague reference to the "preservation of the structure of property relations" begins to lose its usefulness. Why is it, that in advancing the notion of the public interest against the unrestrained contest between capital and labor, the state is serving the interests of the former? Would it not have served capital's interests better simply to crush labor's growing powers? Who could say with assurance that such an offensive would have failed at that time? Further, looking at this from another angle, why was this development — which conceded to organized labor a permanent place at the table where interest-group negotiations would occur — not *also* in the interest of both organized labor and the other types of social interests? Certainly it would not be in labor's interest if we presume that (1) the only truly worthy objective for the labor movement consisted in becoming the dominant social interest in accordance with the traditional socialist vision, and (2) the new developments would hinder the attainment of this objective. Should we, however, consider those to be reasonable presumptions?

Macpherson's own text shows that over the following quarter-century in Britain the idea of the public interest as something separate from and superior to the aims of any other social group took hold in the theory and practice of the union movement and its political arm, the Labour Party. For example, during the debates on the Emergency Powers Act of 1920 almost the entire Labour Party

supported the view that "the public" was to be (in Macpherson's words) "looked on as a third party apart from
employers and workers, a third party whose interest it was
the primary duty of the State to protect."[10] During this
same period the actions and policies of the trade union
movement in Britain showed their increasingly firm commitment to the same path, namely, forcing the state
(through their economic and political power) to ac-
knowledge a duty to uphold and gradually improve a minimum standard of socio-economic benefits — minimum
wages and working condition standards, pensions and
health benefits, unemployment insurance, a "welfare floor,"
greater public amenities, and so forth — and to make many
of these benefits universally applicable. In other words,
labor would not seek to replace capital as the dominant
social interest, but rather gradually seek to diminish the
latter's previously unchallengeable sway over the conditions of social life.

As Macpherson indicates, this strategy obtained even
during the General Strike in 1926, which "was not directed in any way to the supersession of capitalism." The strike
was another tactic, an extreme one justified by the circumstances of the moment; but it was not meant to call into
question labor's overall strategy, which was based on "co-
operation with the employers' organizations with a view
to rationalizing industries on a national scale and securing for the workers a share in the control of industry."[11]
This meant participation on nationwide boards for ongoing consultation between capital and labor, including measures to improve the economic efficiency of certain
industries. In the minds of many this was still consistent
with the eventual triumph of socialism, but in terms of
priorities this long-term goal clearly was to be subordinate
to the more immediate aims of first, protecting workers'
achieved standards of living and levels of social benefits,
and second, bringing about further improvements in the
same.

Allied to this principle was another of equal importance, namely eschewing violence as a means to social

change. With economic collapse clearly evident, the members of the annual meeting of the Trades Union Congress in 1934 passed a resolution pledging the movement to uphold democracy and political freedoms and to work against violence and dictatorship. Macpherson even wonders how firm the union movement's support of the Labour Party program of that period was for centralized economic planning and the nationalization of basic industries and the financial system.

Another side of this "social contract" is the willingness of the state step by step to assume responsibility for an increasing number of matters relevant to the workers' situation for which the unions themselves earlier had had to provide, such as unemployment and health benefits, labor exchanges, legal enforcement of collective agreements, accident insurance, and so forth. Macpherson observes that inevitably such undertakings by the state weaken the union movement in equivalent measure, since the "interest" of the individual worker in protecting and enhancing such benefits is transferred from one arena (unions) to another (the political process).

The great underlying significance of this step is as follows. When the state, as the agent of the "general interest" in society, accepts responsibility for a set of conditions (for example, working conditions) which plays a large part in the lives of the citizenry, and which formerly was regarded from a legal standpoint as a "private" matter, that set of conditions is transferred from the private to the public realm, thereafter to become an element in the political process. While other institutions such as unions might retain their own commitment to improved working conditions, expressed by pressure-group tactics on politicians, their own members discover that now they have in many respects a direct interest in the outcome of political events but only an indirect interest in the fate of the union movement. Writing in 1935 Macpherson states: "The driving force and active spirit of the unions will not survive this change undiminished."[12]

There is a convenient and brief way of highlighting this

kind of development. Regarding the case at hand, we can say that society has "politicized" the issue of working conditions. Although Macpherson does not say it in this way, the observation is consistent with his discussion. Furthermore, in politicizing working conditions, *society to some extent also politicizes the issue of property relations*, because the former (society) acts as a limitation on the scope of the discretionary power and authority formerly enjoyed by the latter (property relations). To be sure, one can reply that it is actually in the "best interest" of the propertied classes for the state to get them to go along, willingly or not (that is, whether or not those classes are "conscious" of what is "objectively" in their own interests).

This reply will hold as long as it is thought that the choice facing all social classes is, in the final analysis, a straightforward "either-or": capitalism or socialism. In the former, the means of production — and thus (according to an influential way of thinking) the determining aspect of social and political life — are appropriated by a small group as private property. The essential program in the latter, on the other hand, is to "socialize" the means of production, as a set of collective goods held for the benefit of all citizens, in some appropriate form — ownership and/or management of all such goods by the state, by workers' co-operatives, by local communes, or in the anarchist version by means of spontaneous associations without the exercise of state authority.

Nevertheless, this "either-or," so self-evident to so many members of various social classes in many parts of the globe in the nineteenth and twentieth centuries, has perhaps vanished for good within much of the sphere of "advanced" or "managed" capitalism (Western Europe and North America). If so, *in contemporary society we have neither private property in the means of production, nor socialized property, but rather politicized property.* This means that we have neither capitalism nor socialism in the traditional nineteenth-century senses (nor are we likely to have either in the future), but rather a hybrid form created by the long historical tension between the other two.

I will outline the essential features of this hybrid in the last chapter.

It was not unreasonable for Macpherson, writing in 1935, to assume that the polarized opposition between capitalism and socialism represented the limits of actual political choices and that no other possibilities were at hand. Although this is not stated directly in his thesis, it is implied throughout; for example, in the section on the British Medical Association he writes: "Wherever their real interest may lie in the future as between a capitalist or a socialist society, it is not surprising that they should now believe their interest to be with the maintenance of a capitalist society."[13] Nonetheless, a third way indeed had emerged in the preceding decade, and he could hardly ignore the model of fascism as another arrangement for "resolving" the opposition between capital and labor. As Macpherson's analysis proceeds it becomes clear that the possibility of a fascist "solution" in Britain is the basis for his evident concern about the emerging social contract between capital, labor, and the state.

As we have seen, for some time before 1935 the trade union movement had sought to become a full partner in a social contract whereby it would negotiate the future state of industrial development with the representatives of capital, under the broad authority of the state, while the state assumed direct responsibility for a wide range of programs affecting working conditions and social benefits. Furthermore, had the Labour Party program been successful, it would have brought large sections of finance and industry under the direct ownership or control of the state, further strengthening (through the union movement's influence on the party) labor's hand in the tripartite relation. Macpherson believed strongly that this would be an intrinsically highly unstable state of affairs, however: this would constitute in his terms a "semi-socialist" state, a political order that would be unlikely to accomplish a transition to "full socialism."

It would be unstable largely because it would enact measures sufficient to thoroughly frighten the existing propertied class without either dispossessing or disenfranchising that class. In Macpherson's view three factors in the situation of the property-owning class would be decisive. First, this class "would retain substantial control over the sources of public opinion," presumably the press; second, it would of course also still be the single most influential interest-group in industry; and third, the class of small business owners (often referred to as the "petty bourgeoisie," although Macpherson does not use the phrase) would be utterly frightened of and hostile to the semi-socialist state. He concludes:

> If the combined incidence of these three factors resulted in the downfall of the Labour Government through the forms of democracy, the succeeding government in its attempt to make the rule of property secure would find an industrial structure whose form expedited a transformation to a Fascist state, and a trade union movement without sufficient power to resist that change. And it is probable that in the stage of social and industrial development that would then have been reached, no other technique than the Fascist one would be sufficient to ensure both the continued productivity of industry and the maintenance of control in the State by the property-owning class.[14]

It must be admitted that this was not an entirely improbable scenario, given the temper of the times. When the "downfall of the Labour Government" actually occurred in 1951, however, the entire historical context had changed, and the remainder of this hypothetical script was not played out.

I am interested in the way this scenario was crafted not in order to assess how well or how poorly it represented the historical possibilities of those times. Rather, an appreciation of what Macpherson's master's thesis tells us about his intellectual formation is important for quite different reasons. In the first place, it is interesting that in his very first foray (as a young man of twenty-four years) as a commentator on issues in social and political theory, he directed his theoretical exposition so explicitly towards a pragmatic end, namely a reckoning of the likelihood of fascism's success in Britain. Second, the presuppositions inherent in his own standpoint, as well as the way in which his key concepts are employed in this first major venture, are indicative of much of his later work.

The main presupposition in his standpoint is the existence of an "either-or" choice between polarized opposites in so far as the basic direction of social change is concerned. As suggested earlier, it is unsurprising that a young, politically-aware theorist of humane inclinations should, in 1935, define the issue of future directions in social change as a choice between capitalism and socialism. Perhaps it is equally unsurprising, given the great peril in which Western societies stood then, that a commitment to a certain standpoint cast under such circumstances should form the secure and unquestioned framework for a lifetime's effort. In any case, a form of argument grounded in polarized choices is a hallmark of all of Macpherson's later work.

For instance, there is the well-known contrast between acquisitive and developmental powers. To take another example, the title essay in his book *The Rise and Fall of Economic Justice* (1985) presents the present possibilities for future social development in terms of two basic options: a "corporatist state" that would destroy the democratic process, on the one hand, and a state based on democratic forces which would "take control of the capitalist state and transcend or transform our present managed capitalism," on the other (but we are not told what it would be transformed *into*).[15] Or, in the marvelous essay entitled "The Economic Penetration of Political Theory" first published in 1978, the choice is represented as being between a "market-dominated" *versus* a "non-market-dominated" society; the former is evidently the one we live in now, but once again the nature of the latter is unspecified. To be sure, this type of exposition often is nothing more than the work of the theorist's bulldozer, which is used to clear quickly the intellectual landscape so that the operator's own new growth may flourish. Fair enough: but in the examples just cited the characteristics of the alternative society indicated by his contrasting pairs are so sketchily drawn that one scarcely knows whether it is worth nurturing.

There is another aspect in which the form and substance of Macpherson's master's thesis presages the distinctive intellectual style of all his later work. The concept of property relations, which is the cornerstone of his thesis, is a theme that he returned to again and again during his career; for example, there are short essays on this subject written in the late 1970s. His treatment of this notion in the thesis is interesting largely as an early illustration of how Macpherson as a political theorist would put a key concept "into play," employing it as a touchstone or reference-point rather than as a specimen to be dissected and minutely examined for the argument he wished to advance. Despite the repeated use of "the structure of property relations" and similar phrases throughout the three hundred pages of the thesis, we are no closer at the end than we were at the beginning to discovering what the author thinks are the constituents of this "structure"! There is no mention of the type of property that is being referred to, the relative importance of different types of holdings (land, securities, etc.), the actual social distribution of wealth, patterns of inheritance, capital investment flows in Britain or elsewhere, or of changes over time in all these and other dimensions.

Eventually his blithe indifference to detail proves costly. In the concluding chapter Macpherson states pointedly that the "underlying property structure . . . makes the society what it is," and then rephrases once again his major presupposition: "For the State's primary function is the protection of the society it knows, a society based on a certain structure of property relations." Until this point reference had been made only to modern Britain. But now we learn that this presupposition is a general one:

> It is not only in a capitalist society that the State
> exists chiefly to safeguard the existing system of
> property relations. That is equally the function
> of the State in any other type of society that we
> have yet known. It is not less true of Russia to-
> day than of any country where society is based
> on the institution of private ownership of the
> means of production.[16]

There follows an elliptical, teasing reference to the utopian possibility of a future society of universal fairness in
which no one would have an interest in altering the distribution of property rights.

Now, a proposition of such generality (applying to all
known types of human societies) is liable to be of limited
utility. In fact, if it were to be taken at face value the author's
own labors in the preceding 300 pages would have been
a tedious and quite unnecessary elaboration of an already
known and established truth. The fact that it is neither
a truth nor a truism, but rather a presupposition against
which the theorist, who wishes to put it into play first,
should have mounted a skeptical assault, is shown soon
thereafter by the author himself:

> The example of the U.S.S.R. shows that the
> totalitarian form is no less necessary in a new
> and still insecure socialist society than in a threa-
> tened capitalist society [such as Italy, Germany,
> and Austria]. For, as we have said, the State in
> any society is primarily the guardian of the sys-
> tem of property relationships in that society, and
> will therefore in any society need power to the
> exclusion of all other associations to the extent
> that that structure is threatened.[17]

Obviously it is not self-evident that, whatever the structure of property relations was in the Soviet Union in the

1930s, such a structure, whether is was menaced from outside its borders or not, absolutely *required* a totalitarian state to "protect" it: on the contrary, the Stalinist state came close to destroying the economy and society of the Soviet Union.

Once again, I want to reiterate that I am not asking whether Macpherson is right or wrong in either his approach to his subject or his conclusions. Indeed it would be churlish to endeavor to find fault with a graduate-school composition that the author never sought to publish! Rather, it is *the form of the argument itself to which I call attention*. That is to say, the concept of property relations, although it appears to be the centerpiece of the argument here, is instead the backdrop against which the real issue of concern to him — the implications of the theory and practice of the trade union movement for the future of socialism in Britain — is presented. This does not mean that the concept itself is unimportant to the author; as noted earlier, Macpherson returns to the notion of property again and again later. The point is, this concept is present in the text to serve a specific function, namely to put into play an argument about what the history of the relations between the trade unions and the state in Britain meant for the prospects of socialism.

In his thesis Macpherson was practicing the craft of the political theorist, a craft at which he would become exceptionally skillful in later years. The essence of his technique, as developed there, was to employ a key concept or a set of polarized appositions which themselves are only sketchily explained as a backdrop against which to examine a whole range of familiar figures and ideas in the history of modern political thought. The best example occurs in the book which made him famous, *The Political Theory of Possessive Individualism*: the key concept of possessive individualism is defined in only two pages towards the end, but in his foregoing disquisition on seventeenth-century English political thought that concept had served as a touchstone by which to take a new measure of what was thought by most observers to be an already well-surveyed terrain.

Foundations 1936-1942

Macpherson's name first appeared in print in a series of four or five brief book reviews written for a short-lived radical magazine published in Toronto. *New Frontier,* "a monthly magazine of literature and social criticism," was inaugurated in April 1936 and was edited by Dorothy Livesay, Leo Kennedy, and others; a successor to *Masses*, it lasted little more than a year. It was an attempt to form a "united front" movement in Canada among the writers' and artists' communities. And it seems to have been doomed from the start, judging from the blast of criticism against the whole orientation of the magazine from Graham Spry, then the editor of the *Canadian Forum*, which the editors of *New Frontier* had the courage to publish in their inaugural issue. Spry clearly thought that any so-called "united front" venture sooner or later would wind up under the control of the Communist Party.

The first issue also contains, among other things, short stories about depression-era themes by A. M. Klein and Mary Quayle Innis, and a short piece by Felix Walter entitled "The Universities and the Depression." Walter referred to a "wholesale persecution" of professors for ideological reasons in the United States at places such as the University of Pittsburgh, but he also remarked that "few professors in Canada have actually suffered for their teaching," although some have been "warned and gagged." Walter says that on the whole Canadian professors are not likely to be radicals — but even less so are the students they encounter!

Certainly the young Macpherson does not appear to have been concerned about the company he was keeping in those days, despite the fact that he was in the first year of his academic career. He had a review of a book about Mussolini (written for a "popular" audience) in the first issue, another dealing with a pamphlet consisting of speeches by Soviet leaders (he did not find this to be particularly useful), and two or three others before the magazine's demise in 1937. Of interest, if the published bibliographic record is accurate, Macpherson changed the orientation of his writing in 1937 and remained faithful thereafter to this decision. After 1937 almost all his output dealt with matters of academic interest and was written for an academic audience; also about ninety percent of his book reviews after 1937 were published in established academic journals, the remainder appearing mostly in established semi-academic periodicals.

His very first "academic" piece is, of all things, a long review-essay on Pareto's *General Sociology* published in the *Canadian Journal of Economics and Political Science* in 1937 (the largest single group of his reviews would be published in *CJEPS* and one of its successors, the *Canadian Journal of Political Science*). Here we find the first instance of what would become a hallmark of Macpherson's intellectual style in his reviews, namely an extensive and careful paraphrase of another author's arguments followed by a critical assessment. The whole is marked by a judicious and evenhanded tone, the sign of one who takes seriously the liberal values of the contest of opinion and freedom of expression. Also, it is clear that Macpherson made a division in his writing as a whole, concentrating in his essays and books on the development of his own views, including a forceful give-and-take with the directly relevant secondary literature, while evaluating works of a more general interest in his field in his regular book reviews.

The review of Pareto's book includes ten full pages of paraphrase and analysis, written in the wonderfully clear and flowing prose style that Macpherson had perfected already (which is no simple task when Pareto is the subject). This review is interesting for its strong concluding remarks on the nature of the social sciences, by way of his objecting to Pareto's tendentious appeal to natural-science methodologies for the study of society. For in the social sciences, Macpherson states, "the observer is a part of the total social situation all or part of which he is observing. His whole attitude is shaped to some extent by the mental climate of his group and his period,..." There is no such thing as complete impartiality in the social sciences, which depend on an explicit sense of purpose and on value judgements in order to give meaning and significance to their endeavors. He concludes this initial academic sally with what is evidently a statement of his own standpoint: "For to understand social problems, which are human problems, one must be of them, not outside them. And to be of them one must share some sense of purpose."[18]

His next piece is equally of interest, for it shows that Macpherson had at the outset of his career a perception of the developing field of political science in Canada as a whole and the place of his own specialty (political theory) within it. The occasion was the publication in 1938 of a *Festschrift* for the man who had hired him, E. J. Urwick, edited by Innis and also containing essays by Bladen and Clark. Entitled "On the Study of Politics in Canada," Macpherson's essay reviewed the development of the field in Canadian universities, with special reference to the British traditions that heavily influenced Canada, and traced its gradual emancipation from other disciplines (philosophy, history, law, and economics). When he drafted his essay, there were only three courses in politics offered at the University of Toronto — a survey course in the history of political ideas, advanced political theory (contemporary theories of the state), and the relation between the state and the economy — but shortly thereafter three courses on government were added.

Macpherson's essay included references to a wide range of works written since 1875 on the government and constitutional history of Britain, the United States, and Canada. He noted the "comparatively late appearance" in Canada of the study of government and attributed this "partly to the late development of a Canadian national consciousness and partly to the fact that the similarity of the Canadian to the English and United States systems of government made a specifically Canadian study seem relatively unnecessary." Likewise he explained the narrow range of Canadian political science studies until then as the result of the domination of the field by scholars trained in Great Britain, who were interested — as far as Canada was concerned — mainly in Canada's distinctive constitutional features, those being "first, the Canadian federal system of government, and second, the fact of Dominion self-government within British imperial unity."[19]

He welcomed recent trends in political science for the attention they were beginning to bestow on the more "concrete" aspects of political structures and processes (noting the influence of American scholarship in this regard). He also urged specialists to concentrate on "recent developments in the Canadian political system," and the areas he mentioned just happened to be those on which he had focussed his master's thesis: the role of the state and its administrative functions and the relation between the state and voluntary associations. In the conclusion, however, he sought to go much further and to carve out a major role for political theory within the field of political science as a whole:

> For nothing in the modern state is to be fully understood unless that state is seen as a product of the interaction of men's ideas and men's actions and the circumstances from which these have arisen and with which they have been confronted. This understanding must be sought in the study of the history of political ideas, considered not as abstract philosophies but as, at each stage, both cause and effect of political, social, and economic situations and activity.[20]

In fact, this "study of the development in interaction of political ideas and concrete political facts offers a new principle of unity" for the discipline of political science. Macpherson demonstrates here a clear sense of mission as a young scholar who is committed not only to an academic career, but also to bring a sense of social purpose to his own discipline. It is political theory itself, properly understood as the study of the interaction of ideas and events, which is to inculcate this sense of purpose by lending an element of unity to an otherwise disconnected set of researches. When this prospect was announced, political science in Canada had not yet emerged as a distinctive discipline (it was not until 1968 that the *Canadian Journal of Political Science/Revue canadienne de science politique* separated from its economics partner in *CJEPS*, for example). The prominent position of theory within Canadian political science today, I suspect, is due at least in part to Macpherson's lifelong dedication to his mission.

His absorption in academic pursuits is shown clearly here, but Macpherson did not hesitate to state at about the same time, and equally forcefully, his belief in the need for social change. A review in 1941 in the *Canadian Journal of Economics and Political Science* of what appears to be a pedestrian volume on the role of public opinion in American politics afforded him the opportunity to make the following straightforward comment:

> Democracy and dictatorship are not the static opposites which the author's emphasis on the importance of their differences seems to imply. The basis of the democracy we have now was established two and three centuries ago by periods of dictatorship or something very like it, and another such period may be required to make our present democracy complete or to make it serve the ends which the people desire. Whether such dictatorship may be required or not depends presumably on whether or not the requirements of the capitalist economy become incompatible with the democratic expression of the demands of the classes which capitalism engenders.[21]

This strikes me as an uncharacteristic remark, perhaps reflecting the strain occasioned by the outbreak of the

long-threatened war following upon a long period of economic crisis. Considering especially the rather staid publication in which it was offered, I cannot help but think
that there is a touch of deliberate bravado in this gesture.
In any case a year later Macpherson, reviewing Gaetano
Mosca's *The Ruling Class*, returned to the same forum to
defend the prospect of socialism: "There is nothing [in
Mosca's argument] to show that, given the socialist institutions of property and the absence of classes whose power is based on ownership of property, the existence of the
mechanically necessary governing class is incompatible
with a greater measure of democracy and equality."

Later that same year he returned to *CJEPS* with a
review-essay on seven new books on political thought.
One or two remarks therein are important as a corrective
to the comment on dictatorship quoted above, and as an
indication of Macpherson's ongoing concern with the fate
of liberalism. He writes: "For those at least who value the
basic elements of the liberal and democratic philosophies,
it is more important now than at any time in the last
hundred years to investigate the conditions for their effective maintenance." The context makes it clear that he
includes himself in the reference. Later, he clarifies the reason for his concern about the future of democracy: since
individualism traditionally is held to be the basis of
democracy, how can it "outlive the disappearance of economic individualism everywhere"?[22] (This is quite similar to the questions that Horkheimer and Marcuse had
posed in their essays of the 1930s on liberalism, but of
course Macpherson would have been unaware of them
then.) The net result of these defenses for both the socialist and the liberal-democratic traditions was to leave
the connection between them unclear.

Suitably enough, Macpherson addressed just this point
in his next major essay, "The Meaning of Economic
Democracy" (1942), written for the *University of Toronto Quarterly*. He begins by defining economic democracy as "an economic order which would make possible the
realization of the purposes or values which political

democracy can no longer realize by itself"; in fact the concept is also and at the same time a political program, a set of "proposals for such rearrangements of the relations between capital and labour and the state as the proponents believe necessary to make democracy real."[23] The need for such a program is based on what was the "conventional" radical critique of capitalist society's institutional structures, namely that great concentrations of property wealth and economic power effectively negate the promised equality of opportunity. Although Macpherson does not cite it, there are echoes here of R. H. Tawney's powerful treatise *Equality* (1931).

More significant, however, are the impacts of these structures on the political process: through controlling information flows (via ownership of the press), political parties, and pressure groups (here Macpherson refers to voluntary associations again), propertied interests ensure that the formal equality of democratic voting power will not upset the established state of affairs. Macpherson sums this up in terms of the "underlying antagonism between democracy and the concentration of property" in modern society, an antagonism whose full social impact was not felt until the twentieth century, having been delayed due to extraneous circumstances (the existence of an open frontier in America and the wealth derived from the overseas empire in England).

This much is conventional: Macpherson concedes that the dependence of political on economic power has been a commonplace since Aristotle. More interesting — in terms of what would actually happen in the postwar period — is his conception of what might be called the permanent state of underlying social crisis under capitalism. As it is usually presented in the radical theory, this is the threat that at any time both the demands made through the political process by the working class for a greater or a predominant share of wealth and power, on the one hand, and the desire of the propertied class to retain its existing privileges, on the other, will be pressed so forcefully that a violent confrontation must result. The key element is the notion of significant change in the relative *shares* of wealth and power. Macpherson does not phrase the point in this way. Instead, he speaks of a theoretical "limit" to the "concessions" that the propertied class will make, noting that this "limit is likely to be reached at the point where the expectations of both classes cannot be met out of a no longer sufficiently expanding economy."[24]

Many Marxist theorists have occupied themselves indefinitely to little profit in laying bets just when such a limit would be reached. The prospects of significant peacetime economic expansion must have seemed remote after the experience of the 1930s. Nonetheless in the Western world during the quarter-century after 1945 the sustained rise in real incomes did indeed lift the whole "social platform" upwards dramatically in terms of material prosperity, while leaving the relative shares of the various social strata intact. In the process, the entire basis for any polarization of society into two classes contending for supremacy collapsed, almost certainly never to return.

In another respect Macpherson's discussion of economic democracy touched on a key aspect of future social change. He conceded that any program on behalf of economic democracy inevitably would increase the role of the state in the economy, and he pointed to the positive experiences already gained with special wartime bodies (such as price and supply control boards), which were generally praised, to suggest that society as a whole need not fear this prospect overmuch. The greater concentration of political power, he suggests, could be offset by a widespread use of advisory and consultative boards, with representatives of all affected groups among their membership, so as to dilute somewhat the authority of centralized bureaucracies. In fact the role of the state in the peacetime economy grew enormously after 1945, although in ways quite at variance with the ones Macpherson identified; and it seems reasonably clear from comments in his later writings that he did not think much progress in achieving economic democracy has been achieved thereby. I will return to this theme in the concluding chapter.

His essay also briefly mentions the concept of industrial democracy, that is, the participation of workers in the management of industry. This is done chiefly to defend the practices of trade unions, including demands for the closed shop, as being consistent with democratic freedoms. His lengthy treatment of this issue can be compared with his curt dismissal in a footnote of the "co-operative movement" as being relatively unimportant, a judgment made shortly before the national impact of the Co-operative Commonwealth Federation peaked. This comparison illustrates Macpherson's commitment to a general theory of modern society in which variations in national events (such as the role of the CCF in Canadian politics), although not wholly insignificant, were not allowed to call into question any major presuppositions of the theory.

"The Meaning of Economic Democracy" is also noteworthy for Macpherson's career in that it introduced two of the concepts, "capacities" and "self-development," on which his later interpretation and criticisms of the liberal tradition would be founded. They were introduced as composing the basic postulate of democracy: stated positively, that each person has a right to live his life "as fully as his capacities allow, always, of course, so far as is consistent with others having the same right"; alternatively, that each person should have "equal access with others to the means of self-development." The need to ensure equality of such access is the basis of what is sometimes called the positive theory of democracy, as opposed to a program dedicated only to removing all obstacles to individual initiative, without regard for the inequalities that afford some individuals a differential advantage in prosecuting their initiatives. Macpherson states his adherence to the positive theory, which views the end or purpose of democracy as "the provision of the conditions for individual self-development."[25]

In the same year (1942) he wrote a second essay on his conception of his discipline. "The Position of Political Science" was published in English in the French-language Quebec journal *Culture*. To the best of my knowledge it is the only source for a direct statement by Macpherson of what I have called his dual commitment.

The special nature of this essay is apparent at once in the epigraphs, since Macpherson rarely used this device: a tame passage from John Stuart Mill is followed by the notorious "thesis" by Marx on the need for changing the world rather than only interpreting it. There is a hard edge to this essay, predicting as it does the rise to prominence within political science of a "class-interest approach," which is said to be appropriate since the two-part class division (capital and labor) within Canada will be increasingly evident as the war continues. Macpherson sees the United States and Canada as continuing to be relatively backward in comparison to European capitalist societies, and attributes this to the "extent and variety" of agricultural interests, which cause sectional divisions to be regarded as more important than class ones. The major change he anticipates is for a labor party to become a leading force in national politics; here one can detect the impact of his stay in England on his outlook for his native country.

A social and political philosophy that is appropriate for these new conditions, that is, one that is "worked out in terms of broad class interests," is needed — "even in Canada," Macpherson adds. This is true in part because the range of established political philosophies is inadequate to the task. In particular liberalism suffers from a

> contradiction which is likely to be explosive — the contradiction which has come to exist between free economic enterprise and other freedoms usually described as democratic. The exigencies of the war may submerge these disputes but a successful end to the war will sharpen them and bring them to a head.

The first sentence in this passage is provided with a footnote reference to "The Meaning of Economic Democracy." This formulation of the tension or contradiction between economic freedom (capitalism or the "fully market society") and political freedom (the ideals of positive democracy) was to be a fixture in Macpherson's thought thereafter.

Almost immediately following this apocalyptic vision an abrupt change in both the substance and tone of the essay occurs. The passage reproduced below is its entire concluding section:

> This leads us to the consideration, which must be brief, of the second and related problem selected for comment. What should be the political scientist's attitude towards the political and social reality he tries to analyse? Should he attempt, in Marx's phrase, to change the world or should he only interpret it? While some will say that is a delusion of grandeur for Canadian political scientists to think that they may choose to "change the world," the choice does confront them, however indirectly. The criterion for this choice must be the furtherance of knowledge; if the political scientist is stampeded uncritically by the clamorous urgency of current affairs he abandons his special function. But this is not to say that the political scientist must eschew a philosophy which calls for an effort to change. On the contrary, as has been argued above, the advancement of a science, its emergence to the second stage, depends on the working out of a philosophy to meet new social needs, a philosophy which informs and is informed by particular investigations. Such a philosophy *ex hypothesi* demands change. Adam Smith and Bentham, Burke and Marx, advanced their sciences because they demanded change. They were solid thinkers; they were also pamphleteers. What is the *Wealth of Nations* but an extraordinary pamphlet — extraordinary for the depth and width of perception its author developed in working out and forcibly stating his so-

cial and economic philosophy?

The political scientist, then, can be at the same time a scholar and a protagonist of a political philosophy demanding change, and he will be a better scholar if he is a protagonist of, or is feeling his way towards, a more adequate philosophy. This does not mean, of course, that the political scientist has to be a politician or a publicist; there is a difference between a journalist and a pamphleteer. Neither does it mean that the political scientist cannot be a politician or a publicist. Scholarship and fairly intensive political activity are certainly not incompatible but they have so far rarely been carried on successfully together.

In less dangerous times than these, it is less difficult for the political scientist to put the advancement of knowledge first, and to wait for the indirect effects of such efforts to contribute to the social changes he deems desirable. The question which disturbs the political scientist now is whether he can afford to wait. There is unfortunately no way to settle this question. The writer can only record his view that the present emergency requires of the political scientist most of all a deepening and strengthening of his philosophy in the light of the new problems and especially the class issues which are likely to become increasingly important in Canada. The political scientist's researches are in any case informed by a purpose and an approach based on whatever degree of general understanding of the world he can get. The approach is going to make all the difference in the research; the research can if kept up deepen and widen his understanding and so strengthen, if necessary by modifying, his approach and his philosophy.[26]

This passage and the essay itself ends with four lines from Thomas Hardy: "No auguring mind can doubt that deeds which root/In steadfast purpose only, will effect/Deliverance from a world-calamity/As dark as any in the vaults of Time." It is a marvelous testament and *profession de foi* from a thirty-one-year-old author; and although the sense of urgency is obviously derived from the war-time situation, the conception of the person who is "at the same time a scholar and a protagonist of a political philosophy" is not. Rather, this conception expresses Macpherson's deepest sense of life and purpose and as well gives voice to the idea of political theory as a vocation. It is the finest part of the legacy from his work.

Development 1943-1954

One could say that the foregoing has revealed a good deal more of the protagonist than the scholar. Fortunately, the credibility of my interpretation is rescued by the very next article on Macpherson's chronological bibliography, which serves it so well that the article might be viewed as having been invented for this very purpose. "Sir William Temple, Political Scientist?", published in the *Canadian Journal of Economics and Political Science* in 1943, is the only truly and completely tedious piece of writing from Macpherson's hands that I have ever read. What is important in this context is both the subject-matter and the style. This is his first published study in the history of ideas, and his subject (a writer of the late seventeenth century) is treated entirely on its own terms, with no references to the issues of Macpherson's day. Moreover, it is entirely faithful to the scholar's craft as it is usually exercised, being virtually a model of pedantry. The year 1943 thus marks the turning-point in Macpherson's practice of the vocation of political theory. Thereafter the balance of his effort would shift decisively to studies in the historical development of political ideas and movements, and the political scientist as protagonist would appear primarily in the lists of scholarship.

By 1945 he was immersed in the literature of seventeenth-century English political thought, the study of which culminated in the book that made him widely known outside Canada for the first time, *The Political Theory of Possessive Individualism* (1962). In 1945 he published in *CJEPS* a review of two collections of Leveller tracts, discussing some of the themes that would reappear later in chapter 3 of *Possessive Individualism* and in his subsequent spirited debates with other scholars (such as essay XII in his collection *Democratic Theory*). In the same year and in the same academic journal the article "Hobbes Today" (reprinted without change thirty years later in *Democratic Theory* under the title "Hobbes' Bourgeois Man") appeared.

His essay on Hobbes shows that he was widely reading both original and secondary sources for the period, but it was also framed in terms of Hobbes's relevance for the understanding of the institutional structures of contemporary capitalism — in other words, it displays the unity of scholar and protagonist once again. There is also an unmistakeable tone of self-confidence and maturity in the writing, illustrated by the following remark: "We would do well to be afraid of Hobbes; he knows too much about us."[27] An interesting sidelight is that we frequently encounter the phrase "bourgeois society," which so far as I know he had not employed in print before, a phrase that normally — at least in a North American setting — marked those using it as a Marxist of one sort or another. Appropriately enough, therefore, we find Hobbes's theory of society being interpreted here through Marx's concept of commodity fetishism. His exposition of the meaning of this concept is exceedingly brief and unsatisfactory, however. In any event the salient point is that this approach was dropped in the later and lengthy study of Hobbes that opens *Possessive Individualism*.

But the main theme itself, namely that Hobbes's scheme of political and philosophical thought is saturated with "bourgeois assumptions," is not especially well argued and in fact depends for its cogency upon the fuller exposition given in an earlier study by the well-known conservative scholar Leo Strauss, *The Political Philosophy of Hobbes* (1936), which Macpherson cites a number of times. This alliance of conservative and radical interpreters is odd but not unfamiliar; Macpherson wished to put a different slant on the results. When he returned to Hobbes in *Possessive Individualism* he had substituted his own terminology, anchored in the concept of the "possessive market model of society," for the tendentious phrase "bourgeois assumptions."

Obviously this was not a substantially different approach, and it still afforded him the purchase he had always sought for launching in the conclusion to *Possessive Individualism* a critique of contemporary society on the basis of his historical study of English political thought. The new terminology, however, allowed him to stay much closer to the language and spirit of the seventeenth-century texts he was examining and to avoid making imaginative leaps of dubious plausibility, such as the assertion in the 1945 essay that Hobbes had a "consistent picture of bourgeois society." As a result the later version became a more forceful and convincing account.

During the decade after 1945 Macpherson consolidated both his academic interests and his commitment to the academic discipline of political science. With respect to the former, he concentrated on two areas, the history of liberalism and the analysis of social credit doctrines. The extent of his activities related to his discipline throughout the 1950s leaves no doubt that he monitored the events happening in his profession, both in Canada and elsewhere. He worked for a number of years on a project supported by UNESCO which resulted in a report for the International Political Science Association that was published in 1954 in the *American Political Science Review* under the title, "World Trends in Political Science Research." The very brief report on Canada therein was supplemented by a separate study also published (in French only, so far as I can determine) in 1954, which was a more elaborate survey of the Canadian scene — this time including Quebec — than was the one he did in 1938.

He continued to observe his own and related academic disciplines and this is evidenced by an essay on the social sciences for a collection entitled *The Culture of Contemporary Canada* (1957) and by the entry for "Political Science" in the *Encyclopedia Canadiana* (1958). Preparation of such articles naturally required wide reading in purely academic sources, reflecting his full-time involvement with the idioms of university life.

His preoccupation with the history of liberalism was recorded for this period in two major essays on Locke for the *Western Political Quarterly*, "Locke on Capitalist Appropriation" (1951) and "The Social Bearing of Locke's Political Theory" (1954), both of which were later incorporated into *Possessive Individualism*. It is also apparent in his series of reviews on the Cambridge University Press's complete edition of Ricardo's *Works and Correspondence*. This preoccupation culminates in the first exposition of the idea of possessive individualism in an essay for the *Cambridge Journal* entitled "The Deceptive Task of Political Theory" (1954). The three propositions that make up this idea — actually he refers to it here as an "assumption" made by liberal theory from Hobbes to Bentham — are: (1) each person is the proprietor of his or her own capacities and is free to employ them in the search for a means of satisfaction, which become possessions — thus freedom is possession (a corollary asserts that this freedom, converting capacities into means of satisfaction, is expressed as the domination over things); (2) the relations of exchange among individuals with respect to their possessions are the basic form of social relations; (3) all rights, including rights to life and liberty, may thus be regarded as property (possession) rights, and the chief end of political action is the protection of the same.

With this idea Macpherson found a *single, unified dimension* in which the interrelationships among all the notions that had been central to his way of thinking so far (property, the marketplace, equality, liberty, and, by extension, democracy) could be displayed. Presenting this unity as a "model" — as he did in *Possessive Individualism* — allowed Macpherson to be suitably imprecise about whether he was referring to theories about human behavior, on the one hand, or the actual record of historical events, on the other. (As a matter of fact, as I will show in the next chapter, it suited his purpose to slide back and forth between these two domains.)

The second advantage gained through this expression is that, by virtue of the unity imparted to the elements that compose it, Macpherson could display that ensemble effectively as a "real" dynamic and historical process, rather than as a static collection of more or less interesting ideas. He did this by the simple device of suggesting that an assumption such as possessive individualism changes its meaning and function with changes in society: the same individualist assumption which "was the strength of the liberal theory in the seventeenth and eighteenth centuries (when it corresponded with the social reality) ... became the defect of that theory about mid-nineteenth century (when it ceased to do so)."[28] The point of the device was to chastise liberalism for failing to see that the original synthesis of property and individual liberty had collapsed by the middle of the nineteenth century under the growing concentration of economic power brought by capitalism, and that a "new class consciousness" (presumably the working class is being referred to) necessarily had rejected liberal values on that account.

Thus, the conclusion to "The Deceptive Task of Political Theory" stays faithful to the basic outlook that had characterized Macpherson's work until this point. However, by the time when the interpretive scheme, grounded in the notion of possessive individualism, was elaborated in his 1962 book, the conclusions had been altered dramatically — indeed, the earlier one was rejected in favor of a quite different position. In the passage from the 1954 article quoted just above Macpherson says that possessive individualist assumptions had ceased to correspond with social reality already by the middle of the nineteenth century. In his book, however, Macpherson conceded that the "assumptions of possessive individualism ... still do correspond to our society, and so must be kept."[29] This concession meant that his earlier critique of liberalism should have been completely overhauled; but the conclusions to *The Political Theory of Possessive Individualism* avoided this task, offering in its stead only the rather weak complaint that no theory of political obligation for contemporary society can be founded on the old assumptions of possessive individualism.

The essence of what Macpherson considered to be the "dilemma" handed down in the legacy of liberal theory was, as we have seen, the tension or contradiction between property and individual freedom. His concession that in the mid-twentieth-century possessive individualist assumptions still corresponded with social reality meant that there was no apparent contradiction between property and individual freedom, however. Thus, the abandonment of his earlier position in 1962 had left him without a firm basis for a critique of either liberalism or contemporary society. He was able to re-establish his critical position only when he reconceptualized the notion of property some time later: subsuming property rights under the category of human rights, rather than setting property and liberty in opposition as he had been wont to do, permitted him to develop a new and original basis for the critique of existing social arrangements. This new point of departure will be followed more closely in the next chapter.

Now we must consider Macpherson's other major project of this period, his study of the political theory and practice of the Social Credit Movement. Macpherson dealt with this first purely as a theoretical venture, publishing "The Political Theory of Social Credit" in *CJEPS* in 1949. He used his readings in European social theory to advantage for the first time in this piece, noting the parallels in social credit doctrine with themes in writings by the nineteenth-century thinkers: Fourier, Saint-Simon, and Proudhon. Well over half of his article is devoted to summarizing the views of social credit's originator, Major C.

H. Douglas, and Macpherson again shows here (as he did in his review-essay on Pareto) a remarkable capacity for presenting another thinker's position, even and indeed especially when he disagrees with it, in concise, fair, and lucid terms; in fact the result appears to be an improvement upon the original.

The assessment of the political significance of the Social Credit Movement that he developed in this article would be carried over intact to *Democracy in Alberta*. The main issue discussed was the movement's challenge to the traditional party system and its success in maintaining power in what was for all intents and purposes a one-party environment. Macpherson attacked the Social Credit form of one-party politics without taking refuge in the conventional "liberal" standpoint that a multi-party system is a requisite for democracy. Thus he refers to historical examples of what he calls "one-class democracies" (which may have one party or none), citing as examples the regimes led by Cromwell, Robespierre, and Lenin; a regime may be called democratic, he says, if it promotes "the moral, intellectual, and active worth of all individuals," that is, "if it releases the productive force of society from previous obstacles and if it develops wide participation in administration, as was notable in the examples just mentioned."[30] These highly provocative — and ultimately indefensible — remarks might have been more convincing to his academic audience had he paused at that point in order to marshal some evidence on their behalf.

One-party movements are attempts to submerge and overcome social class divisions, Macpherson says. They inevitably fail to do so when they overlook the real basis of those divisions and instead focus on some arbitrary aspect of the whole, such as finance capital (as both social credit and some fascist movements did). This opens up the road to dictatorship, "for by seeking or pretending to remove the evils of which they complain by credit reform alone, they fail to resolve the class tension which, if not moderated by the democratic party system, can only be covered over by plebiscitarian dictatorship."[31] This

passage was reproduced almost verbatim in the concluding chapter of *Democracy in Alberta* ("plebiscitarian dictatorship" was replaced by the phrase "the devices of a
plebiscitarian state"), showing that the analyses in both article and book led to precisely the same point.

The much longer treatment of Social Credit in
Democracy in Alberta is important for reasons other than
a comparison of the end-points towards which the arguments proceeded. During the decade of the 1950s, as indicated above, Macpherson spent much time and effort
in keeping tabs on the full range of work in his academic
discipline of political science, and in his own book he immersed the discussion of social credit doctrines in the
wider context of Canadian political history. His training
and early teaching experience embraced comparative
government as well as theory, and he himself reported in
conversation that he was intrigued by the Social Credit
Movement because it was an oddity, at least so far as the
nations of the British Commonwealth were concerned,
with respect to its notion of government (particularly its
opposition to cabinet government). The extent of empirical detail contained in the book about Alberta's social
structure, party documents, and political history is un-
paralleled in all of Macpherson's published writings.

Finally, however, that empirical detail was not allowed
to constitute a rigorous test for the explanatory power of
key concepts, especially the concept of social class. In a
moment I will try to explain why this was the case and
what its consequences were.

When William Aberhart's Social Credit League won 89
percent of the seats in the 1935 provincial election, Alberta was actually beginning the second phase of its long
infatuation with non-party or one-party political systems.
The United Farmers of Alberta (UFA) had started the first
phase by winning office in 1921, a phase that continued
uninterrupted for fourteen years, whereupon the UFA
movement disappeared from the political scene in 1935
as quickly as it had emerged. Both the UFA and Social
Credit Movements opposed cabinet-dominated govern-

ments and advocated a "populist" control over the movement's organizational apparatus and political platforms by elected delegates.

Social Credit doctrine originated in the writings of an Englishman, Major C. H. Douglas, that began to appear in print around 1920. His economic theory was based on the idea that the main obstacle to social well-being was the control over the supply of money and credit by the great financial institutions. The result, according to Douglas, was that people did not have sufficient wherewithal to purchase what they needed. Major Douglas's remedy was to advocate the issuance of a "national dividend" in the form of credit slips that would enable people to increase their purchasing power. Needless to say, the remedy was never implemented by the political organizations in Western Canada that came to power under the Social Credit banner. In Alberta, for example, although Major Douglas was under contract as a consultant to the government, Premier Aberhart began rejecting his advice as soon as he took office.

Macpherson's main line of interpretation in *Democracy in Alberta* can be summarized as follows.[32] He attributes the uniqueness of political life on Canada's Western prairies (presumably he is referring to Manitoba, Saskatchewan and Alberta, but this simple matter is never made clear) to two factors, namely the "relatively homogeneous" social composition of the population and the "quasi-colonial" relations between that region and the rest of Canada. The latter point is reasonably well-known, having to do with the tariff, resource, and transportation policies imposed on the West by federal governments, while the former is much more important for his argument. Macpherson seeks to establish it with the aid of empirical data on Alberta's working population: in 1941 farmers and other "independent commodity producers" constituted 45% of the province's employed persons, while "industrial workers" made up 41%; this is contrasted with the national average for Canada, namely 30% and 60% respectively. No comparison with Saskatchewan is ever offered, nor does Macpherson examine the reasons for which the political histories of Alberta and Saskatchewan deviated so sharply in this period (the difference is noted once only in passing in a footnote, but never explored); since one must assume that the two prairie provinces had a very similar social composition, this omission is both curious and damaging to his interpretation.

The political programs of Social Credit and its one-party predecessor, the United Farmers of Alberta, are explained simply as the outcome of a false presumption that the interests of all groups were identical with those of the independent commodity producers — in effect, they assumed that in one sense or another all persons were such producers. Thus, the Social Credit objective was to unify this group, so that its members would not compete against each other, and to have it speak with one voice. What others may have regarded as substantial differences among groups, such as differences between the interests of farmers and industrial workers, were simply ignored by these movements.

Macpherson gives a concise account of the basis for the self-consciousness of independent commodity producers, such as farmers, who are engaged directly in the work of transforming the physical environment, and who can usually see the completed results of their labor in the form of goods that are useful and necessary for the satisfaction of immediate needs. All obstacles the producers encounter in maximizing the output of their labor, and that arise from social relations, such as unreasonably low prices or high interest and transportation charges, appear as "artificial" barriers to well-being and fruits of conspiracies plotted by parasitical and unproductive groups. (The impediments result from willful evil, unlike natural calamities such as drought and pestilence.) Since the causes of their malaise are straightforward, the proposed remedies are thought to be equally uncomplicated.

In terms of the standard political vocabulary these remedies are "radical" in some respects and "conservative" in others. Macpherson explains this state of perpetual oscillation between the two poles of the political sphere as the outcome of the peculiar situation of the Canadian prairies, where a regional concentration of a particular group (independent commodity producers) existed in a quasi-colonial relation to their own national government.[33] Their radicalism stemmed from their wish to rebel against Ottawa, and their conservatism arose from the fact that they, as independent producers who thought that they could and should control the means of their production, had a direct interest in property rights. The appropriate term for the members of this class, whose lives are dominated by the struggle to defend their property in the midst of great economic insecurity and the accumulating impacts of the economic concentration growing all around them, is *petit-bourgeois*. Their situation is defined most precisely by their inability to identify themselves with either one of the two decisive classes in capitalist society, labor and capital; and their unwillingness to recognize the fact that they are a marginal group in modern society gives rise to the false consciousness of the class.

At the very end of his book Macpherson introduces a new term, the "quasi-party system," that serves to summarize the political expression of this class. The Western Canadian experience could not be described accurately enough as the operation of either a non-party or a one-party system, although its main thrust was to attack the traditional form of multi-party politics. It rather became a quasi-party system, one in which a dominant, nontraditional party (usually set in opposition to the main national parties) existed among the weakened remnants of other political parties, providing a middle way between the normal state of democratic politics and the authoritarianism of a true one-party state.

The American sociologist Seymour Martin Lipset wrote a long review of *Democracy in Alberta* for the *Canadian Forum* in 1954. Lipset had published *Agrarian Socialism*, his study of the Saskatchewan CCF, in 1950, which was a revision of his doctoral thesis done under Robert S. Lynd's supervision at Columbia University. Lipset wrote

a touching dedication to his book ("to the memory of my
father, Max Lipset, who had the same dreams as the farmers of Saskatchewan"), as well as a preface in which he
identified himself as a supporter of "the democratic socialist movement of which the CCF is a part" and expressed his gratitude for the warmth and kindness with
which he, a young man who had not previously travelled
more than a few miles west of New York City's Hudson
River, had been received by farmers and others in Saskatchewan when he undertook his field research there. One
might suppose that Macpherson would have looked kindly
upon that work, with its obvious sympathy towards its
subject-matter (even the by then well-known and appropriately conservative Lipset who wrote the 1967 preface to
the republication of his book displays a lingering sympathy). Yet *Agrarian Socialism* is not even mentioned in
Democracy in Alberta.

In his *Canadian Forum* review Lipset objected that
Macpherson had not given good grounds for holding his
major presupposition, namely that differences in systems
of political parties could be explained by differences in
the composition of social classes. He claims that as a generalization it would not stand the test of a comparative inquiry into Canada, the United States, and Europe, and that
even for Alberta it was not a strong hypothesis, since a
"winner-take-all" form of voting, in a setting where patterns in political affiliations were distributed evenly
throughout the ridings in the whole province (as they often
have been in Western Canada), could place one party in
office for a long time even when strong opposition to the
ruling party existed among the electorate. Lipset did not
deny that a direct relation between parties and classes
could occur, for he conceded that such a relation existed
in Britain; but not in Canada, Lipset thought, since Canada was more like the United States or France with respect
to the relations between social groupings, political parties,
and government.

Macpherson's spirited reply is valuable chiefly for its
straightforward restatement of his main working assump-

tions, especially those dealing with the concept of social class: "My assumptions were that classes have class interests, and have class positions which set limits to the policies which might succeed; that classes are more or less conscious of their position; and that with historical hindsight we can try to say whether their consciousness of their position at any turning point in their history was more or less accurate,..."[34] So far as his central argument about Alberta itself is concerned, he restated what is said almost in passing towards the end of *Democracy in Alberta*, that "both the working-class and the bourgeoisie have, at crucial periods in their history, displayed a greater awareness of their class position and needs than the *petite-bourgeoisie* has generally done,..." Furthermore, Macpherson had also explicitly defended his adherence to the concept of class as the "most penetrating basis of classification for the understanding of political behaviour," despite the fact (as he notes) that most scholars in his discipline, even those who had earlier found it useful, were abandoning it in favor of concepts that were more amenable to "techniques of measurement and tabulation."[35]

We can now understand why Macpherson had found no succor in *Agrarian Socialism*, despite its author's ideological sympathy with the CCF, for Lipset's argument was that North America was unique in the modern world because much of its struggles for social improvement had stemmed from longstanding traditions of agrarian radicalism. This is not to deny that substantial numbers among the urban working class at various times and places committed to radical change and socialist ideologies; but it had become apparent over time that these commitments were neither as deep nor as enduring as they were in many other places in the world. Many political leaders had also tried to unite the radicalism of farmer and urban labor groups, with very limited success. Such an effort at unification had also been made in the early days of the CCF in Saskatchewan, but as Lipset had shown in detail, by the mid-1930s the CCF began to abandon explicit references to socialism in its political tracts, because most of the farm popu-

lation simply would not accept a political program for radical economic and social change based on socialist
ideology.

The view that most demands for radical social change
in Canada had emerged (and were likely to continue to
do so) from a non-ideological radicalism, that is, from tem-
porary alliances of social interests which did not derive
their impetus from the confrontation of the two allegedly dominant classes of bourgeoisie and workers, was simply unacceptable to Macpherson. Nevertheless, to phrase
the point plainly, in this he was wrong: his concepts of
class and class consciousness could not adequately
represent events. Lipset's looser "sociological" categories
grasped better the actual range of diverse social interests
as well as the political awareness and objectives of various groups in the social movements he and Macpherson
were examining; and with them can be understood the
earlier contest in the prairies between the CCF and Social
Credit for the allegiance of the rural population, the con-
trasts between federal and provincial voting results, and
the later swings in voting patterns there between conservative parties and the New Democratic Party.

People and groups do not normally occupy fixed
points on a political spectrum. Rather — at least starting
from the time when most people have some minimal
"stake" in society to protect, or even only the hope of having the same — their objectives embrace both their attempts to preserve that stake (which is their conservatism),
on the one hand, and whatever measures they believe may
be necessary to improve their position (which is their
progressivism or radicalism), on the other. Where the
majority will stand in terms of support for political parties and their programs at any time, therefore, depends on
how it will assess the balance of its interests in the light
of the circumstances of the moment.

As Macpherson's own argument shows so well, his approach was defective not so much in the concept of class
as in the concept of class consciousness. After conceding
the point in his reply to Lipset that neither he nor anyone

else believed that all members of a class could hold the same view, he took refuge in the last redoubt of all defenders of the notion of class consciousness, namely in the claim that (unlike the theorist) members of a class may not understand their own class interests. This expedient, which derived its currency in twentieth-century critical theory largely from the force of Georg Lukacs's great essay on reification, gradually collapsed of its own weight; so far as I know, Macpherson did not use it again. The concept of class has been with us since the days of ancient Greek political theory and, given a sensible statement of its meaning, most social thinkers find it useful; but the notion of class consciousness — the presumption that commonality in material circumstances is or must be matched by a specific interpretation of the meaning of those circumstances — has been much less successful in winning adherents, chiefly because to give a plausible account of what a "true" consciousness might be has been a more arduous task than it first seemed.

Since the conceptual apparatus for *Democracy in Alberta* was flawed, the prognosis drawn from this study could not stand the test of time. In the book's conclusion, Macpherson extrapolated Alberta's situation to Canada as a whole, arguing that, just as this province stood in a quasi-colonial relation to the nation, so the nation stood in a similar relation to the United States; moreover the "characteristic independent-producer assumptions about the nature of society are very widespread in Canada, a legacy of the not distant days when anyone could set up in business or farming for himself."[36] Thus he predicted that the political expression of this situation that had arisen in Alberta — the quasi-party system — would triumph in Canadian federal politics as well. When his book was republished a decade later, he noted in the new preface that this conclusion had gained more attention than had the rest of the book! He maintained in 1962 that the course of federal politics in the preceding period fully justified his position. Events thereafter, however, tell a different story.

Macpherson did not repeat this attempt to bring his powerful design for dealing with issues in political theory to bear on an extensive analysis of political events. The role he had forecast for political theory in his 1938 essay, "On the Study of Politics in Canada" (through a "study of the development in interaction of political ideas and concrete political facts"), indicates that political theory would offer "a new principle of unity" to the discipline of political science.[37] *Democracy in Alberta* unfortunately does not weather the test of his own criterion, which would have required him to directly confront the kind of empirical detail given in Lipset's 1950 study of the neighboring province that appeared at the very time when he was preparing his book on Alberta. Had he thus addressed "the development in interaction of political ideas and concrete political facts" in the political history of the Prairie Provinces he would have been forced (I think) to amend both his working assumptions and his conclusions, both of which were based on an unsupportable view of class and class-consciousness. For there was no "working class" in the classical mold (as a clear numerical majority in society with a unified and distinctive set of political goals) that existed in Canada in 1935, nor was there any good reason for Macpherson to suppose at the time of writing his book on Alberta that such a class would come into being in this country in the future.

Any decent survey of "concrete political facts" — recall his disparaging reference to "techniques of measurement and tabulation" in his reply to Lipset — would have confirmed the point. In the absence of this concrete dimension, the other half of the partnership ("political ideas" or theory) had to attempt to bear unaided the weight of the elaborate and strained exercise about class consciousness that brings *Democracy in Alberta* to its conclusion.

The load was too great: *Democracy in Alberta* was a dead-end for Macpherson. He never again tried this kind of unifying study of theory and practice that he had imagined at the outset of his career, a type of study that would represent the distinctive contribution of his own academic specialization (political theory) to the discipline of political science. When he returned to the lists a decade later with *The Political Theory of Possessive Individualism*, he did so by adopting the standpoint of epic theory in the grand style.

3

Maturity: 1955 to 1985

The Scholar as Protagonist

Throughout his formative period, Macpherson structured the various issues in political theory and practice with which he dealt largely in terms of an opposition: capitalism *versus* socialism. Whether the matter at hand was trade union practices or the theory of property, social credit politics or the fate of liberalism, each illustrated for him the continued viability of the one overriding set of options that had been posed in the mid-nineteenth-century and had been forcefully posited anew for his generation by a series of fateful events — the Bolshevik seizure of power in the Soviet Union, worldwide economic crisis, and the rise of fascism.

At mid-career, beginning in the late 1950s, the explicit posing of issues in terms of this opposition in his writings was muted, which does not imply any fundamental change in his views: the terminology was a bit different but the main point was pretty much the same. Certainly others saw him this way, as we know owing to the increasing amount of attention paid to his work both in Canada and abroad. Many of his followers regarded him as a Marxist of one sort or another (in one evaluation he was assessed as "five-sixths" of a full Marxist[1]), and his harshest critics all labeled him with assurance a socialist, despite the fact that he stubbornly refused any ideological label.

My treatment of Macpherson's formative period in the preceding chapter suggested that he had embraced a dual commitment to academic scholarship and to social improvement as an undergraduate and that he never wavered thereafter. Yet these were never meant to be two parallel but separate tracks. Their unity, as presented in Macpherson's 1942 essay "The Position of Political Science," makes it quite clear that the scholar was to serve the protagonist; the image of their unity is the pamphleteer, and Adam Smith is referred to as a model. The roles of both scholar and protagonist — the terms are his own, from the 1942 essay — were to be played with equal seriousness and honest effort, for in Macpherson's eyes the protagonist could be served by the scholar only if the latter role were played strictly according to the tenets of the academic profession. We have also seen how closely he followed and reported on the progress of purely academic scholarship in his periodic reviews of the developments in his discipline of political science.

Macpherson's subsequent career shows that each side of the scholar-protagonist duality subsisted in an unstable and problematic relation to the other. The serious commitment to the scholar's craft placed a heavy toll on the partnership, requiring in fact that by far the greater portion of available time be spent in its service, and, moreover that this time be devoted to activities such as wide reading in historical source material whose fruits would have no *direct* bearing on contemporary issues. Of course, the protagonist's concerns were never overlooked; the book reviews, minor essays, and comments in major works reveal Macpherson's continued devotion to this side of the partnership. Nevertheless, the fact that comparatively little time was left to him either for sustained exposition or sustained research in new sources of information on political institutions and "concrete political facts" is evident in the record of his published writings.

After 1960 Macpherson's steadily growing reputation within university circles both at home and abroad was partly responsible for ensuring that the balance would remain tipped towards the concerns of scholarship. Beginning with the reviews in learned journals of *The Political Theory of Possessive Individualism*, other scholars took increasing notice of his work and inevitably (for this is the scholar's staff of life) mounted spirited attacks on substantive points both in the interpretation of sources and on Macpherson's presumed standpoint. So far as I know, Macpherson never missed an opportunity to reply to any major review or commentary (nor did he ever concede a significant point to a critic); and in all those replies he remained faithful to his 1942 statement that the scholar could only serve the protagonist by being a good scholar. For example, in answering Jacob Viner's long review of *Possessive Individualism*, in which Viner highlighted what he regarded as a Marxist interpretation, Macpherson made this public affirmation:

> I am equally astonished at Viner's final complaint that the book has an "apostolic" purpose which prevents its being as high a contribution to scholarship as it could otherwise have been.... I do not recognize that [Marxist apostolic] fervour in myself or in my book, and I reject the imputation ... that any of my readings of the texts are, presumably because of such fervour, perversions of the texts.... By making Marxism a spectre he has ruled out all the intellectual insight which is still to be had from the original Marx, and has weakened the prospects of scholarship by creating a disjunction where

none need exist.[2]

Since the calibre of his writing drew eminent and learned critics into the lists, his determination to defend himself according to all of the accepted canons of scholarly inquiry forced him to continue to pay close attention to the *minutiae* of historical scholarship.

During the 1960s his standing in his profession was also recognized in a series of honorific posts such as the presidency of the Canadian Political Science Association and the Canadian Association of University Teachers, speeches at convocation exercises, and prominent roles in a series of formal inquiries into allegations of professional improprieties at various Canadian universities. In addition, he participated in the reviews and controversies about the governance of universities that were prompted by the the student protest movements of the time. Some of these activities were time-consuming and unrewarding, but they were also a natural outcome of his lifelong mission to work within a university setting.

I mentioned above that for the young Macpherson, the scholar was meant to serve the protagonist, and I have suggested that in the actual course of events the amount of actual service rendered by the former to the latter was quite limited. (Once again there is an interesting parallel with, although no influence from, the leading members of the Frankfurt School. The remarkable series of essays written in the 1930s by Horkheimer and Marcuse especially, which are breathtaking in the scope of their learning and the daring quality of their insights, are similarly the products of scholar-protagonists who were committed to the cause of socialism. Horkheimer and Marcuse, however, were so fully and passionately devoted to learned discourse that the practical political lessons they sought to draw therefrom were almost impossible to fathom!) What about assistance to the scholar, however? Was it possible in Macpherson's case for the protagonist to serve the scholar?

Certainly this was the case in his own eyes. The 1942 essay suggests that scholarship would be stronger if it were imbued with a sense of purpose derived from a "general understanding of the world" (but he also concedes that the results of research in turn may modify the protagonist's outlook); and in his reply to Viner he notes that scholarship is weakened if ideological bias disallows the testimony that a particular thinker may have to offer. The second claim is a strong one, but the first is not particularly convincing: the criterion for the "sense of purpose" is too vague, and plenty of good scholarship is produced by academics who have no other purpose in mind save turning out the very best research that they can.

On the other hand, a number of his fellow scholars took exception to his approach to scholarship for a variety of reasons and with varying degrees of outrage. Macpherson replied in kind, and for years these sharp exchanges added some spice to what were otherwise rather dull periodicals; surely this was not his ultimate purpose, however. What then was his purpose? In what ways could the protagonist's cause be advanced by means of scholarship?

To take one example: At the very end of *Possessive Individualism*, following almost three hundred pages of detailed commentary on seventeenth-century English political thought, we are told for the first time that the assumptions of possessive individualism are "now morally offensive" — and the adverb is very important, for the point is that such assumptions were not morally offensive in the seventeenth century, but became so in the nineteenth and remained that way thereafter. This, however, is not what the book itself is all about. The book is devoted to ascertaining whether the writings of English political thinkers from Hobbes to Locke can be said to have been shot through with the assumptions of possessive individualism. Macpherson answered his question in the affirmative and many other scholars demurred, most of them doing so by seeking to limit the impact of this interpretation (saying it was strong for Locke and the Levellers but weak for Hobbes, for example). As I have noted, this is the conventional stuff of academic life.

The curious feature of all this, of course, is that accepting Macpherson's version of history holus bolus would do absolutely nothing for the claim that the possessive individualist assumptions are "now morally offensive." This may indeed be the case, but no case had been made for it. The claim was not a trivial one, since it implied that the determining feature of contemporary society (the marketplace) is at stake; thus the claim seemingly would have deserved a treatment at appropriate length, perhaps a book in itself, in which reasons for and against its legitimacy could have been considered fully. Macpherson never wrote such a book, confining himself instead to short sections on this point in some of his post-1965 essays. Thus in this case, Macpherson's scholarship was simply irrelevant, if a justification of his own claim about the moral offensiveness of possessive individualist assumptions was *really* at stake: the scholar did nothing for the protagonist's cause here.

Did the scholar perhaps benefit the protagonist indirectly rather than directly? Certainly his strong commitment to the university setting, and the sheer amount of effort devoted to those scholarly debates in which only specialists could participate, limited severely the extent to which his critique of society could spread beyond the walls of academe: the debates conducted in its idioms perforce would go unnoticed elsewhere. Also his explicit standpoint as a protagonist may have curtailed some of the influence he would have had otherwise with respect to the purely academic interests of his specialist peer group in political theory. Thus this conclusion about the relation of scholar and protagonist in Macpherson's career is the same as the one arrived at earlier, namely that the latter was of limited service to the former.

Yet, however limited, it did serve. On balance his determination and skill in scholarly research and debate, and his high standing in his profession resulting therefrom, caused his own concerns to be placed squarely on the agenda for his discipline of political theory in Canada for a number of years. Although these things are hard to measure, I believe that Macpherson did succeed in considerably broadening the range of academic debate within political science in Canada and elsewhere. In so doing he, and others who agreed with him, also brought his standpoint on contemporary society — that a market society was based on morally offensive assumptions — forcefully before large numbers of students.

The impact was felt all the more because the function of the university setting where scholarship is performed changed quite dramatically over the course of Macpherson's long career. Not only were Canadian universities tradition-bound institutions when Macpherson entered their service; universities in Canada and elsewhere were traditional elitist institutions then, serving a comparatively small proportion of the population as a whole, a proportion drawn primarily from overwhelmingly male and upper-income segments. The universities' social role, apart from advancing knowledge, was largely confined to regulating entry into the professions and the civil service. We must recall again that these were times of widespread despair and foreboding in society at large, and thus for a young academic to launch his mission as scholar-protagonist in such surroundings took a good deal of courage. Given the special circumstances of the times, it was not unreasonable for him to hope that the acceptance of such a mission by himself and others might succeed in marshalling the university's resources and prestige on behalf of the struggle for a better society.

The economic prosperity and social changes that had been accumulating in the postwar period spilled over into university life in the 1960s. Sheer numbers, for one thing; a far more diverse student body; a social consensus that part of this prosperity would be devoted to public purposes, such as better education and health care based on a principle of universal access. All this also affected the social function of the university: a changing economy demanded wider proficiency in general skills for white-collar occupations, and a university education would now be a standard requirement for entry into them. The period of upheaval caused by the "student movement" was dramatic but relatively brief; however, it had a lasting impact on the conduct of university affairs.

By now, the notion that one can be both scholar and protagonist is widely (although not universally) accepted within universities, precisely in the terms that Macpherson proposed in 1942: one must be *both* scholar and protagonist, accepting the responsibilities of each role in the fullest sense, and become better at both by allowing experience gained in each to inform and improve the other. Naturally one cannot attribute the existence of this consensus solely to the example of Macpherson and others of his generation, but it is not unreasonable to suppose that he had a large part to play in bringing it about. Long after the learned debates about the presence of possessive individualist assumptions in the works of the seventeenth-century English political theorists have become mere curiosities of intellectual history, this contribution will be making its effects felt in the practice of academic activity in Canadian universities.

Five Themes

Since I am concentrating primarily on the "epic theory" aspects of Macpherson's work in this book, I have confined myself to the major themes in the writings of his mature period, themes that constitute his critique of contemporary society and his suggestions for a better way that arise out of this critique. There are five such themes; all of them are related to each other, and moreover they are internally related in a specific way, so that the five together make up a unified conception which may be displayed as follows:

ECONOMY	MEDIATION	POLITICS
	3 THE	
1 MARKETPLACE	LIBERAL SOCIETY AND	4 PROPERTY
versus	STATE IN	*versus*
2 SELF-DEVELOPMENT	THEORY AND PRACTICE	5 DEMOCRACY

This scheme represents my distillation of Macpherson's basic themes and their relation to each other based on a large number of scattered passages in his publications from 1955 to 1985.

The liberal society and state (usually referred to as liberal-democratic society) is the fundamental mediating force in modern history for Macpherson. It links two decisive developments: first, the activity in the capitalist marketplace, namely the growing predominance of a theory of human essence as infinite appropriator and infinite consumer (together with a corresponding practice in actual life); and second, the struggle within the political order between the social class interests which seek to defend the specific property system based on that theory, and practice of the capitalist marketplace, on the one hand, and those interests which seek to transcend it in the name of a different ideal, on the other. The propertied interests use the party system and other devices (such as control of information) to ensure that the liberal state upholds market principles against the power of majority rule, despite the pervasive inequities and injustices that these principles continue to produce. Other classes and groups use the tradition of civil liberties and due process that are protected by the liberal state to create laws and programs that compensate individuals for some of those injustices, to control the operation of market forces, and also to mount a public advocacy of more radical transformations of the social order.

The mediating role of the liberal society and state is precisely what has allowed a group of modern Western nations to survive the bitter class divisions introduced by capitalism without resorting to the worst excesses of authoritarian rule and internal violence. Through courage and persistence, organized labor and other groups were able to curb and mitigate the operation of market forces against the determined resistance erected by propertied interests. This opposition, however, was unable (and to some extent unwilling) to challenge the bases of the reigning property system, and both inheritance and persistent distributional inequalities insured the perpetuation of a society stratified along lines of wealth and economic power. The ability of propertied interests to use the liberal state to preserve their predominant social position, while conceding the necessity for constraining the market system, gave them, as well as the oppositional groups, a real stake in the maintenance of democratic processes and civil liberties.

There was no inevitability in all this. Most Western nations more than once stood on the brink of accelerating class violence that threatened to turn into civil war, and in response the propertied interests contemplated their chances of permanently suppressing opposition to them by means of an authoritarian state. In return, a determined minority within labor and other organizations sought to overthrow existing institutions, including the liberal state, with whatever means were at hand. That such outcomes were avoided is due as much to chance as it is to any overriding commitment by individuals from all sides to affirming the ideals of the liberal state. Such affirmations are fragile and do not form a secure redoubt for liberal-democratic processes, no matter how many successive generations enjoy their fruits; even today one wonders how severe a test in any period of heightened social tensions those processes would endure.

The published record will show that Macpherson remained faithful to those liberal-democratic ideals, despite an equally strong commitment to what many others saw as the competing or even contradictory ideals of socialism. Thus, preserving the theory and practice of the liberal society and state meant preserving the ongoing tension between the economic and political orders in modern times, a tension that itself was responsible for the progress of modern history through developmental stages and for a gradual improvement in the lot of the majority of persons.

The entire scheme illustrated above is a genuine process of historical mediation, because each of its two "sides" — the spheres of economics and politics respectively, which are discrete, readily identifiable domains of human action — do not stand in simple "opposition" to the other, but rather are themselves (as the diagram shows) a unity of complex forces made up of partially contradictory tendencies. Indeed, this structure of internal opposition is what drives each sphere forward through developmental stages.

So far as the economic sphere is concerned, in the capitalist marketplace economy the predominant conception, as well as the predominant behavior patterns based thereon, is that every individual should seek to maximize utilities, which results in the propensity for appropriation and consumption without natural limit (this is the "possessive individualist assumption"). This proclivity stands in permanent opposition to the individual's striving for self-development. They are the two end-points of a continuum; their relation is inverse, so that an advance along the line for one is a retreat for the other, and vice versa. The position on the line where the social system as a whole stands at any time, then, has a reciprocal impact on the sphere of politics: the relative strength of the possessive individualist assumption will influence or determine the type of social and political demands that the majority will make through the democratic process.

Turning to the political sphere, Macpherson, in one of

his major early essays, "The Meaning of Economic Democracy" (1942), defined the driving force in modern history as the "underlying antagonism between democracy and the concentration of property." In his formative period this was primarily a static opposition: propertied interests used the mechanisms of the liberal state, especially the party system, to thwart the demands for redistribution that would otherwise have been pressed successfully by the majority through democratic processes. This conception remains with Macpherson to some extent, but it also undergoes an interesting transformation, for the tension between property and democracy is dynamic, rather than static. The *meaning* of property is explored more fully during his mature period, and property is revealed to be a basic human right. This result, which stems from the internal workings of the sphere of politics, naturally has a reciprocal impact on the possessive individualist assumptions which drive forward the economic sphere.

Each of these five themes, as well as some of the specific relations among them, will now be examined in greater detail. They represent the scaffolding for the major contributions made by Macpherson in his mature period. The support structure that had been provided during his formative period, namely the opposition between capitalism and socialism, was not discarded; rather, the original supports were dismantled and the materials re-used in a much more elaborate framework. All in all, it became a vantage-point from which to survey a wide range of contemporary issues in both social theory and practice.

Economic Sphere: The Marketplace

Each of the two spheres of economics and politics has two dimensions: the institutional context and the individual context. In the economic sphere the first is represented by the general character of the marketplace, and the second by the inner tension between "appropriation" and "self-development" in the lives of individuals. Since these are not separate phenomena, but rather only two perspectives of the same issue, they will be treated independently, purely for purposes of discussion.

1. The Institutional Context

Comments on what he usually called the "capitalist market society" comprise one of the most consistent threads in the writings of Macpherson's mature period. Although other commentators have taken a different view, it seems to me that this is the point where Macpherson most clearly joins the Marxist tradition: namely, in the presumption that modern society is in its "essence" a social order founded on fully developed market (or commodity) relations, and that it must be replaced by one founded on some qualitatively-different principle of social organization. Given the importance of this theme, it is rather surprising to discover in Macpherson's writings so little descriptive narration on the history, characteristics, and evolution of the economic system of generalized commodity production.

In fact, Macpherson redefined the Marxist approach entirely in his own terms! He did so at the beginning of *The Political Theory of Possessive Individualism*, where he states that the assumptions which comprise the possessive individualist model of the human essence "do correspond substantially to the actual relations of a market society." There are eight such assumptions (or postulates):

(a) There is no authoritative allocation of work.
(b) There is no authoritative provision of rewards for work.
(c) There is no authoritative definition and enforcement of contracts.
(d) All individuals seek rationally to maximize their utilities.
(e) Each individual's capacity to labor is his own property and is alienable.
(f) Land and resources are owned by individuals and are alienable.

(g) Some individuals want a higher level of utilities or power than they have.
(h) Some individuals have more energy, skill, or
possessions than others.

Taken together the eight describe the principles of a "full
market society." His reason for adopting a new terminology is also explained:

> If a single criterion of the possessive market so-
> ciety is wanted it is that man's labour is a com-
> modity, i.e. that a man's energy and skill are his
> own, yet are regarded not as integral parts of his
> personality, but as possessions, the use and dis-
> posal of which he is free to hand over to others
> for a price. It is to emphasize this characteristic
> of the fully market society that I have called it
> the *possessive* market society. Possessive mar-
> ket *society* also implies that where labour has
> become a market commodity, market relations
> so shape or permeate all social relations that it
> may properly be called a market society, not
> merely a market economy.

Note especially that this passage elucidates only two of
the three terms in the key phrase: a specific sense for "market" is not given.[3]

It is a curious omission, given the crucial importance
of the concept of fully developed market relations in Macpherson's thought. Clearly, he assumed that its meaning
was self-evident, in the sense that the earlier tradition of
political economy (both liberal and Marxist) offered ample guidance as to what this concept meant. His own writings contain only offhand remarks that presuppose some
more adequately elaborated argument that is neither given
nor referenced: for example, the claim that the marketplace creates wants and tastes (a credo for critical theory),
or the statement that the "politically conscious working
class" in the nineteenth century undermined the "moral

adequacy" of the assumptions on which market society is based (a proposition that cries out for a few shreds of evidence in its support), are both lacking in argument.

Macpherson paid a heavy price for this neglect. All of the publications in his mature period are riddled with basic ambiguities. Does he mean that the first two terms in the phrase "capitalist market society" are indissolubly linked, so that one must have them both together or have neither, or can we have a system of fully-developed market relations (a "full market society") that is not capitalist? Specifically, is it possible to have a socialist variant of a full market society?

The title itself for one of the essays in the collection *Democratic Theory*, "Problems of a Non-Market Theory of Democracy," implicitly takes the position that "capitalist" and "market" are the same.[4] In addition, the overwhelming predominance of the phrase "capitalist market society" in the writings of the mature period reinforce the view that the two terms are inseparable; no explicit suggestions to the contrary can be found. There are, however, some reasons for believing that Macpherson abandoned that view at some point, and perhaps never did hold it, but instead was guilty of inexact usage.[5] If we assume at the very least that he ceased to hold that view, we are still left without much assistance in his publications for developing what might be called a "positive" theory of the full market society. I shall turn to this task in the following chapter.

In Macpherson's theory of the marketplace we are left with just the basic propositions that labor is a commodity, entailing that persons may alienate their energies and skills for a price, and that market relations "shape or permeate all social relations." His relative disregard of the need for fuller exposition here is compensated for, however, in the richness of the conception he developed for the other side of the economic sphere, the individual context. In one sense the marketplace became the foil for what was counterposed to it, namely the opposition of "extractive versus developmental powers" that was played out in the lives of individuals.

2. The Individual Context

A number of straightforward expressions in Macpherson's works link the marketplace in an inverse relation to the prospects for a richer self-development of individuals. The clearest is at the opening of *The Life and Times of Liberal Democracy*: "I shall suggest that the continuance of anything that can properly be called liberal democracy depends on a downgrading of the market assumptions and an upgrading of the equal right to self-development." In an essay on the same theme written a few years later, he contends that "the possibility of a genuinely participatory democracy emerging in Western liberal-democratic states varies inversely with their electorates' acceptance of system-stability as the overriding value, or (which amounts to the same thing) their acceptance of the possessive individualist model of man."[6] The idea that these two are indeed "the same thing" is not given the benefit of a proper argument.

Macpherson's "developmental ideal" will be sketched briefly below. As he himself has said, this ideal originates in the set of values for liberal-democratic society that John Stuart Mill fashioned in the nineteenth century.[7] The conjuncture of influences from Marx (the critique of market relations) and J. S. Mill (the ideal of individuality) is one of the most interesting features of Macpherson's work. Since he is so reticent about the topic of market relations, Macpherson never explained how and why the capitalist market society could be thought to supply a basis for the emergence of the developmental ideal that had not existed in prior human history. Such an explanation is essential; curiously enough, Marx had given quite a good one. (Macpherson had not used it in working out his own standpoint; the main source, Marx's *Grundrisse*, did not become widely known in the English-speaking world until after the publication of a complete translation in 1973.) The brief recapitulation of it which follows will be helpful for assessing Macpherson's position on the relation between market behavior and individuality.

Marx's *Economic and Philosophic Manuscripts of 1844* (which Macpherson had read in part as an undergraduate) presents a one-sided condemnation of capitalism casting it in entirely negative terms, and envisioning a quick passage beyond it to a better society. By the time he came to write the *Grundrisse* (1857/8), however, Marx's understanding of historical development had changed, and in that work capitalism appears as a necessary presupposition for the eventual emergence of human individuality and freedom. This positive historical mission refers specifically to the situation of the individual in the future — a situation which would exist after capitalism had passed, but which could come into being only because of what capitalism had accomplished:

> The discovery, creation and satisfaction of new needs arising from society itself; the cultivation of all the qualities of the social human being, production of the same in a form as rich as possible in needs, because rich in qualities and relations — production of this being as the most total and universal social product, for, in order to take gratification in a many-sided way, he must be capable of many pleasures, hence cultured to a high degree — is likewise a condition of production founded on capital.

Part of the what he calls the "civilizing influence" of capital, Marx says, is to break down "all traditional, confined, complacent, encrusted satisfactions of present needs."[8] Both geographical barriers and previous static modes of production, he believed, had limited the expression of needs in earlier societies, and this constricted the human capacity for enjoyment and thus human development itself.

Marx relates this civilizing and liberating mission of capitalism to that concept which links his thought directly to John Stuart Mill's: individuality. In the passage quoted above, and elsewhere, he interprets this concept as meaning "universality," that is, as the conditions under which every person can explore the full range of potential human capacities for creativity and enjoyment. According to Marx, capitalism teaches mankind to be dissatisfied with the satisfaction of needs at the level of "mere subsistence" and creates a need to strive beyond that level. In another passage the concepts of individuality and universality are explicitly joined; here Marx also relates them both to the full market exchange economy brought into being by capitalism, and again he insists that capitalism represents a necessary stage in human history:

> Universally developed individuals, whose social (*gesellschaftlich*) relations, as their own communal (*gemeinschaftlich*) relations, are hence also subordinated to their own communal control, are no product of nature, but of history. The degree and the universality of the development of wealth where *this* individuality becomes possible supposes production on the basis of exchange values as a prior condition, whose universality produces not only the alienation of the individual from himself and from others, but also the universality and the comprehensiveness of his relations and capacities.[9]

The main points in Marx's positive theory of market relations may be summarized as follows. (1) Precapitalist societies imposed severe limits on the development of human creative capacities. (2) The new needs that emerge under capitalism are manifestations of a new "general" need of indeterminate scope for production and consumption beyond the point of simple subsistence. (3) These new needs are also an expression of a fuller human personality and of its enhanced capacities for enjoyment. (4) A richness in needing is an essential aspect of individuality and human freedom. (5) Individuality is the comprehensive development of human capacities. (6) The emergence of this type of individuality as a general phenomenon in society presupposes the experience of a society based on full market relations.

Of course there is a negative side as well. While permitting the qualitative and quantitative expansion of needs, the capitalist mode of production imposes its own set of limits and barriers to satisfaction. The principal barrier, that social wealth can only be produced in the form of exchange value, arises out of the very nature of capitalism itself. As Marx puts it in *Capital*, what is produced is determined by what can be produced profitably: The "needs of capital for valorization" stand opposed to and rule over the "needs of workers for development."

What this means is that at any time some people have urgent requirements for the necessities of life (such as food and shelter) that go unanswered, because the goods that would satisfy those requirements cannot be produced and sold for a price that the needy can afford and that will at the same time enable the producer to reap a normal level of profit. If widespread deprivation (malnutrition, inadequate health care and education, and so forth) prevails while already existing productive resources are idled or underutilized by the owners of capital, as was the case during the Great Depression, we can say that there is a conflict between capital's needs and those of individuals. Or, even if there is in general an adequate level of want-satisfaction, it may happen that large numbers of people begin to express demands that cannot be met through the operation of market relations, that is, where goods are priced separately and direct payments from consumers are required. Examples of these non-marketable goods or "direct use values" are seen in health care, education, public transportation, and other goods that are supplied to all individuals on an equal basis (either without charge or at a price that does not cover their costs) and are paid for out of general tax revenues. In this case, a set of goods has been removed from the purview of market relations, so that, in supplying them, no conflict between capital and individuals is allowed to occur as a matter of principle.

Thus, in Marx's complete vision of the capitalist marketplace there is an interesting dynamic tension between its positive and negative aspects that has been played out in practice since Marx's time. In many ways this form of market relations has continued to penetrate previously untouched aspects of social and personal life; on the other hand, in many countries other aspects of life have been insulated completely or partially from the full impacts of market principles. Marx himself could see a resolution of this tension only in the transcendance of capitalism and the implementation of qualitatively different social forms (socialism and communism). Yet as Stanley Moore has shown so well, both the arguments and the descriptions for these new social forms given by Marx were so poorly presented that they could not be regarded as a rational basis for revolutionary programs.[10]

The dialectical tension between positive and negative aspects of fully-developed market relations worked out by Marx is an excellent basis for Macpherson's contrast between extractive and developmental powers, however.

The Economic Sphere: Individuals as Doers and Consumers

The foregoing discussion illustrates how, in Macpherson's view, events that affect the individual context within the economic sphere during centuries of capitalist hegemony might influence the popular view of the relation between marketplace and society. From the beginning he had framed his consideration of market relations in terms of assumptions about the "human essence," that is, about how people ought to behave if they wish to promote and enhance their well-being. Nonetheless, Macpherson never offered a composite sketch for this idea in which all the elements were fitted together; what follows, therefore, is my own attempt to outline it.

In modern history, there is an ongoing tension between two competing "models" of the human essence, each of which presumes to be a comprehensive statement about what humans *are* (by virtue of their very nature — potentially, that is to say) and about how they *should* act (if they wish to fully actualize their innate and unique qualities). Like all other great schemes in political thought, therefore, these are meant to be, at one and the same time, both descriptive and hortatory statements. In order to win any following, however, the schemes must bear some plausible relation to the types of things that we see our fellow humans actually engaged in around us. The models themselves, however, are made up of postulates, not empirical data, and thus they are not subject to the ordinary routines of proof and disproof.

In Macpherson's version the two competing models share a common foundation, namely human beings considered as bundles of capacities and powers. Capacities are "uniquely human attributes"; normally Macpherson resisted any pressure to be more specific than that, but on one occasion he listed them as "the capacity for rational understanding, for moral judgement and action, for aesthetic creation or contemplation, for the emotional activities of friendship and love, and sometimes, for religious experience," adding later the capacity for transforming Nature (which includes "materially productive labour") and for curiosity, laughter, and games. The powers of humans are also simply "their potential for using and developing their uniquely human capacities." Obviously there are other human attributes, but Macpherson thought that these were the desiderata for exerting and developing human capacities. Subsequently, in response to the obvious objection that he had avoided listing any unpleasant qualities, he simply said that the ones he had named are the ones required for a democratic society to be able to function: human capacities "are taken to be only those ... the use and development of which does not prevent others from using and developing theirs."[11] In other words, this is simply the way Macpherson wished to define the concept of human capacities for the purposes of the argument that followed. So far so good.

Different commentators are expected to construct different lists, but no one is likely to deny that those offered by Macpherson belong among the table of human capacities. The two models intervene at this point; let us use Macpherson's labels: "developmental" and "extractive." The former model asserts that, regarding each person's powers — which are the summation of his or her energy, skill, and ability to exert the same — there must be *"access* to whatever things outside [that person] are requisite to that exertion." In other words, the developmental model must "treat as a diminution of a man's powers whatever stands in the way of his realizing his human end, including any limitation of that access." (The point is conceded that any individual's access is quite properly limited by the proviso that resources of equal value must be available for every other person.) The other model may be adduced easily as a variant: the extractive model is the conception of a man's powers that "includes his natural capacities *plus* whatever additional power (means to ensure future gratifications) he has acquired by getting command over the energies and skill of other men, or *minus* whatever part of his energies and skill he has lost to some other men."[12]

These additions and subtractions represent the "net transfer of powers" operating in a capitalist economy that arise because most persons must sell their labor power on unfavorable terms to those who control access to resources for both the means of labor and the satisfaction of needs. The transfer of power has three aspects. The first is that the worker loses the value that s/he adds to a product by his/her labor over and above what s/he is paid in wages — a familiar idea from the Marxist tradition and its notion of surplus value. There are also two other and much broader aspects, which in effect incorporate a theory of freedom and a theory of consciousness within the notion of the transfer of powers. Thus, the second aspect is the diminution of a person's productive powers, defined as the capacity to produce material goods, to the extent to which the person cannot determine for herself or himself the choice of activities on which to exercise those powers.

The third aspect is the diminution of what we may call a person's extra-productive powers, "that is, his ability to engage in all sorts of activities beyond those devoted to the production of goods for consumption, to engage in activities which are simply a direct satisfaction to him as a doer, as an exerter (and enjoyer of the exertion) of his human capacities, and not as a means to other (consumer) satisfactions." Finally, the very important connection between the second and third aspects is made as follows:

> For the presumption is that the way one's capacities are used in the process of production will have some effect on one's ability to use and develop one's capacities outside the process of production. A man whose productive labour is out of his own control, whose work is in that sense mindless, may be expected to be somewhat mindless in the rest of his activities.[13]

(Unfortunately, Macpherson offered no examples of what he meant by "mindless activity.") I will further discuss the doer-consumer contrast later. Here we must examine another contrast that arose in this expanded conception of the transfer of powers, namely the distinction between activities which are ends in themselves and those which are means to other ends.

Such a distinction is another element in the contrast between two views of human capacities: "Whatever the uniquely human attributes are taken to be, in [the developmental] view of man their exertion and development are seen as ends in themselves, a satisfaction in themselves, not simply a means to consumer satisfactions." Macpherson says that this notion has its roots in ancient and medieval political thought and was resurrected in different forms in the nineteenth century by such diverse thinkers as Carlyle, Nietzsche, Ruskin, and Marx; but it owes its prominence as a competing ideal in liberal-democratic theory to John Stuart Mill and his followers. The opposed view sees humans as "a bundle of appetites seeking satisfaction," as utility-maximizing creatures:

> This is the postulate that man is essentially an unlimited desirer of utilities, a creature whose nature is to seek satisfaction of unlimited desires both innate and acquired. The desires could be seen as sensuous or rational or both. What mattered was that their satisfaction required a continuous input of things from outside. Man is essentially an infinite consumer.[14]

This view, given its most complete exposition by Bentham, is the core of the dominant liberal-democratic ideology that runs from Hobbes up to J. S. Mill.

At first glance there seems to be a serious difficulty here. Is the creation of utilities not an absolute necessity for the exertion and enjoyment of human capacities? For by "the creation of utilities" is commonly meant the production of all those things that satisfy human needs, not only so-called basic needs for food, shelter, and so forth, but also the expanded set of needs that define a civilized existence, such as those that give rise to culture, beauty, and a sophisticated palate. The answer to the question posed above is clearly "Yes"; but for Macpherson this does not cancel the opposition between the two models. He seeks to uphold the two-models argument, not by distinguishing utility-*creating* from utility-*maximizing* behavior, which would have required of him some delicate metaphysical exercises, but by maintaining that there are qualitatively-different routes to the same end.

Macpherson states that the two (humans as self-developers *versus* humans as infinite consumers) are not incompatible "in the abstract," that is, considered only as concepts, but they are indeed incompatible in historical reality. This is described in two alternative ways. "First, what is opposed to the maximization of individual human powers is not the maximization of utilities as such, but a certain way of maximizing utilities, namely, a system of market incentives and market morality including the right of unlimited individual appropriation." Thus it is only one particular type of utility-maximizing behavior that causes a blockage of developmental powers; in concrete terms it does so by instituting over time vast inequalities in the distribution of property, leading to a denial of "the equal right of each individual to make the best of himself."[15] And sometimes Macpherson was willing to modify the terms of the opposition, saying that what is opposed to the developmental ideal is not the image of humans as infinite consumers of utilities as such, but only its further extension to humans as infinite appropriators of property — which leads in actuality to the same result of inequality noted above.

We can now see clearly how the later concentration on possessive individualist assumptions leads directly back to the central concept of property in his formative period.

Finally, there is the distinction between "doer" and "consumer," which is simply a variant of what has already been presented, for the doer, who is "an exerter and developer and enjoyer of his human capacities, rather than merely a consumer of utilities," is just another name for the agents of the developmental ideal. This variation, however, provides further clarification for the meaning of the term "consumer" in Macpherson's thought: consumption is a passive rather than active mode of life, and it serves only an incidental or instrumental function with respect to exertion and enjoyment of human capacities.

I will now put all these points together in a matrix that gives an overview of Macpherson's claims with respect to the two models.

CRITERIA	MODEL A DEVELOPMENTAL	MODEL B EXTRACTIVE
Group I: Attributes 1. Exertion and enjoyment of capacities	Full	Limited
2. Powers of each individual	All retained	Net Transfer
3. "Outside Things"	Equal access	Unequal access
Group II: Context 4. Economy	Non-market? [market but non-capitalist?]	Fully market? [capitalist market?]
Group III: Activities 5. Mode of Action	Doing	Consuming
6. Objective of Action	Ends-in-themselves	Means to other ends
7. Satisfaction	Direct	Indirect
8. Self-consciousness	Adequate	Somewhat mindless

There are two points about this matrix requiring comment. First, the question marks at the Group II items refer back to an issue raised in the preceding section, as to whether Macpherson meant to distinguish between a "capitalist market" society and another possible type, which does not now exist but may come into being sometime, namely a society based on a fully-developed set of market relations that operates in some non-capitalist form. This does not affect the account given of the extractive model, but it does have a bearing on how we think about the developmental model. Second, we must recall earlier comments on Macpherson's "method" as an epic theorist, which he uses to uphold the developmental and extractive models as an "either-or" choice. This requires him to highlight the differences between them and to make it appear as if their attributes are fundamentally incompatible;

however, there are other options. For instance, he could
have exhibited his extractive model as another kind of developmental path, thus considering it as an alternative to
(rather than the opposite of) the one he prefers. Instead,
he leaves us with the impression that there are no redeem-
ing features at all in the extractive model, or at least none
worth mentioning. Such a polarization of presuppositions
and choices is perhaps the single most distinctive chararac-
teristic of Macpherson's approach.

When I apply Macphersonian themes to contemporary
society in the concluding chapter, I shall do so on the sup-
position that we cannot accept such a polarization. I maintain there that any future we can foresee for contemporary
society (in particular, for Canada) will include fully-
developed market relations as one of its determining features. Therefore, if we wish to retain the core of Macpherson's developmental idea, as I think we can and should,
we will be forced to revise his account of this idea in order to incorporate within it the operation of market relations. This will require major revisions to the above matrix,
including the criteria of mode of action, objective of action, and satisfaction.

In one of his later works, *The Life and Times of Liberal
Democracy*, Macpherson spoke (with reference to J. S. Mill)
of "the contradiction between capitalist relations of
production as such and the democratic ideal of equal possibility of individual development" and again, more suc-
cinctly, of "a contradiction between capitalist relations of
production as such and the developmental ideal."[16] The
context for these· remarks and others like them makes it
plain that when Macpherson is speaking of capitalism in
this way he is working within a framework of ideal types.
Furthermore, the statements just quoted hold for every
conceptual scheme, value system, or public policy orientation, or every attempt to put any of the foregoing into
practice in economy and society, that is intended to in-
duce people to believe and act as if they were essentially
infinite consumers and infinite appropriators. Let us label
this the "capitalist agenda."

The Capitalist Agenda

Serious challenges to the capitalist agenda have been mounted since the nineteenth century, as Macpherson often notes, and there continues to be strong resistance to it in contemporary society. Can one say that despite such challenges it remains the dominant agenda now — say in Canada? This may be impossible to answer, at least not without having a much more precise definition of the term "capitalist agenda." Macpherson has given insufficient guidance here. The move towards an adequate political framework for the democratic ideal, which in *The Life and Times of Liberal Democracy* is identified as participatory democracy, is said to be blocked by both a preference for "affluence" over "community" and by a belief that our market society can guarantee affluence to most persons. The success of participatory democracy, he says further, is predicated on a "downgrading or abandonment of market assumptions about the nature of man and society," on a reduction of social and economic inequality, and on "a change in people's consciousness (or unconsciousness), from seeing themselves and acting essentially as consumers to seeing themselves and acting as exerters and enjoyers of the exertion and development of their own capacities."[17]

In the next chapter I will return to this point, and ask what happens to Macpherson's scheme if we suppose — as I think we must do now — that most persons in Canada today do see themselves as actually exerting and enjoying their own capacities, at least to some significant extent, and moreover that they certainly do not regard either existing market relations or their consumer behavior as being inconsistent with their present utilization of their capacities. Quite the contrary, in fact. I will argue there that we should respond to this evident state of affairs not by taking refuge in a theory of false consciousness, by supposing that all such persons are blinded by the propaganda of commodities. Rather, we ought to revise aspects of Macpherson's developmental ideal while retaining its "spirit."

It is precisely in all his references to the sphere of consumerism that Macpherson consistently errs. So far as I know, there is in the entirety of his writings no reference to that sphere which even hints that anything worthwhile may transpire there. As an issue, consumerism is framed narrowly to begin with: he wonders whether any level of consumer benefits could compensate for the "work situation of employees in a system of capitalist rationality" and whether workers will ever change their priorities "from consumer satisfaction to work gratification."[18] Whatever answers might be given to these musings is one thing; a more important observation is that Macpherson apparently never considered that consumption activity is in itself a significant domain of human creativity and satisfaction — as an expression of individuality, as a source of diverse and genuine satisfaction, and even as an end in itself. I shall return to this point in the concluding chapter.

One major reason for this blindness is easy to pinpoint. Macpherson was always searching for elements in the tension within the individual context of the economic sphere (doers *versus* consumers) that evidenced resistance to the capitalist agenda. At a certain level of generality such resistance becomes an oppositional political program, and thus the link between economic and political spheres is established. His representation of the difference between doing and consuming ruled out in principle any possibility that under conditions of general affluence consumer activity could aid in enriching the developmental ideal.

What he does unearth in his search for resistance to the capitalist agenda is a rather arbitrarily-chosen assemblage: concern about environmental pollution, community and neighborhood movements, worker participation in management (industrial democracy). Curiously enough, he even includes the factor of "increasing doubts about the ability of corporate capitalism to meet consumer expectations"![19] In reality there is very little unity among the various groups which advance such causes, in their composition, objectives, or methods; nor is it self-evident that the commonality of these causes (apparently, whether their proponents realize it or not) is a striving to "downgrade market assumptions." In sum, Macpherson never showed how there is any specific basis here for the enrichment of the developmental ideal.

The difficulty in describing and assessing Macpherson's account of the economic sphere in his mature period is just this: when he wrote about present-day matters, did he think he was referring to what is still "basically" or "essentially" (despite all modifications since it originated) the capitalist agenda or not? If so, then for anyone who accepts the polarization of options represented in Macpherson's two models the structure of market relations in their capitalist form remains the single most significant obstacle to further social progress.

I think that the answer to the above question is indeed in the affirmative. An essay first published in 1985 says: "It would be idle to speculate on the possible extent and timing of what I have loosely called the transcendence of capitalism. But if and when it comes ...."[20] Certainly, the persistence of large-scale accumulations of capital in the hands of "private" investors, and the decisive influence of these investors' actions in global capital markets, constitute a plausible basis for such an answer. But we ought to look at Macpherson's remarks on issues in the sphere of politics first, and especially at his later reflections on the concept of property, before closing the book on this matter.

The Political Sphere: Property versus Democracy

The two forces held in tension within the political sphere throughout modern history, property and democracy, are so tightly linked in Macpherson's thinking that they must be considered together.

An essay entitled "A Political Theory of Property," first published in his collection *Democratic Theory* (1973), can be regarded as the centerpiece of Macpherson's contribu-

tion to contemporary political thought. Its explicit treatment of changes in the nature of property as a political
issue over the whole course of modern history marks the
resumption in his mature period of a theme that was a cornerstone of his formative years; in the years that followed
he then edited a volume titled *Property* and wrote a number of new essays on the subject. "So all roads lead to
property": the point of convergence for most of the main
currents in his other writings.

There are practical as well as theoretical issues at stake
in his contentious interpretation of liberal-democratic
thought. Macpherson signals his belief in the importance
of property for actual social change thus:

> It may even be that the break-through of cons-
> ciousness ... which would release us from the
> false image of man as infinite consumer and in-
> finite appropriator, will come through a further
> transformation of the notion of property, in-
> duced by changes now already visible in the in-
> stitution of property itself and in the needs
> which it serves.

Thus, the relation to the ideas discussed in the preceding
section is firmly established. Moreover, at the same time
he makes explicit the equally important link to the political sphere, specifically the theory and practice of democracy; for Macpherson "the structure of property relations"
(the expression that is the constant refrain in his master's
thesis) was always the integument enclosing together the
spheres of economics and politics.

The key change in the meaning of property in the
twentieth century is a process of "broadening." The
dominant earlier notion of the right of an individual or
corporation to exclude others from the use of things is
by no means abandoned, but competing notions have
been added, especially the claim to a right of access for
everyone to a minimum share of resources. This share is
in effect an entitlement to a stream of revenue that is suffi-

cient to sustain every person at a decent level of existence, whether this stream of revenue be generated by earning an income at paid employment or receiving various kinds of welfare benefits from the state. This is the idea of property as universal right, a right "to the means of a fully human life," that is is to say,

> (a) a right to a share in political power to control the uses of the amassed capital and the natural resources of the society, and (b), beyond that, a right to a kind of society, a set of power relations throughout the society, essential to a fully human life.

"Political power," he adds, "then becomes the most important kind of property"; and with this statement we arrive at the single most important feature of contemporary political life.[21] Although Macpherson does not use the expression, what he has achieved here is the concept of the *politicization of property*. Some speculations on the broader implications of this concept will be offered in the concluding chapter.

In effect, Macpherson says, the state thereby takes over many of the allocative functions formerly managed by the marketplace, and in so doing severely limits what was hitherto the almost unrestrained sway over property exercised by individuals and corporations. He also recognizes a danger in this assimilation of the economic and political spheres, namely that politics might be regarded as just another forum in which the competition among individuals and groups for control over productive resources occurs. Voters might be regarded as consumers of political programs and public policies, exercising their sovereign power by making choices among them on utility-maximizing grounds. Such a conception did arise in political science, and it offered the devotees of unconstrained market behavior another opportunity to display the alleged explanatory power of their finely-tuned models. Macpherson sought to check this initiative first by applying against it all the objections previously raised against possessive individualist assumptions, and second (and more importantly) by using the normative language of rights.

The essay "Human Rights as Property Rights," first published in 1977, provides an elegant and forceful resolution to the longstanding tension in Macpherson's thought between property and democracy. In his formative period that unresolved tension seemed to have only one possible outcome when the demand for genuine democracy and equal rights was pressed. This was the conventional socialist solution of "abolishing" private property in the means of production, taking it (with or without compensation) from its owners and setting up "socialized" property, which of course meant in practice (except for the anarchists) that it would be owned by the state and managed by the public-sector bureaucracy. Now another way is perceived, contingent upon seeing individual property essentially as "the means to a full and free life of action and enjoyment."

The solution is startling. Through this final conceptual twist, the ultimate aims of democracy and the system of property are no longer opposed but identical. The chances of really bringing this about depend upon our making a basic choice between two competing sets of objectives, and we should not be surprised at finding out what our options are:

> We may just go on behaving as insatiable consumers. Our demand for the means of a full life may just be a demand for more consumer goods. But it need not be so. We may pick up again what is a very old idea, the idea that used to prevail before the market economy converted us all into consumers: the idea that life is for *doing* rather than just *getting*. You may ask, can the right to such a full and free life of action and enjoyment be made an individual property, i.e. a legally enforceable claim that society will enforce in favour of each individual? There is no intrinsic

difficulty about this.[22]

If we take this statement as a kind of terminus for the road that Macpherson travelled during his career, from his earliest comments on property to this radical reformulation of the idea, we can find in it traces of the two main problematic areas in his standpoint.

One has been noted by Steven Lukes, namely the curiously individualist character of Macpherson's utopianism.[23] The developmental ideal is always cast in terms of individual action (or as in the case here, individual property), and the perfunctory allusions to "community" we encounter here and there in his writings do not do justice to the part played by social relations in defining the possibilities for the realization of human capacities. On the other hand, the rejoinder can be made that the mainstream socialist tradition has overemphasized the desirability of social controls on individual action imposed in the name of justice, giving rise to fears that excessive conformism and suppression of civil liberties inevitably will accompany every socialist regime. In this context Macpherson's stress on the fullest possible realization of every individual's capacities, reflecting his unshakeable commitment to the positive side of the liberal-democratic tradition, can be regarded as a beneficial influence.

The other potential difficulty has to do with the stark opposition he posits between doing and consuming. Macpherson can easily accept the idea that much of the capitalist agenda has already been shelved. He can also admit the proposition that liberal-democratic society emerged as part of a historical brood we call "capitalist market society." Seemingly he wishes to pretend, however, that the siblings — chief among them, liberal-democratic institutions and fully-developed market relations — bear no genetic resemblance to each other: "[T]he central ethical principle of liberalism — the freedom of the individual to realize his or her human capacities ... has outgrown its capitalist market envelope and can now live as well or better without it...."[24] It is impossible, however, to discover in Macpherson's writings what this statement actually means, since (as noted earlier) the question as to whether he is referring only to the capitalist form of market relations, or to fully-developed market relations as such, was never clarified.

Yet there is no form of fully-developed market relations that does not entail consuming things, as that activity is normally understood, and therefore Macpherson's straightforward opposition between doing and consuming does suggest that market relations as such are the problem. This impression is strongly reinforced by aspects of his discussion of John Stuart Mill in *The Life and Times of Liberal Democracy*. Certainly it is plain how powerfully Mill's writings influenced Macpherson's core concept, the developmental ideal. On the other hand, he finds fault with Mill's sketch of a better society that would be based on a network of producers' co-operatives, because "the competitive market system would still operate, for the separate co-operative enterprises were expected to compete in the market, and would therefore be driven by the incentive of desire for individual gain." Note that, in fairness, Mill's scheme should not be considered as a variant of the capitalist agenda, because the economy would not be directed by a class composed of a small minority of persons who dominate the productive system through their control over capital resources. Despite this Macpherson continues:

> In other words, Mill accepted and supported a system which required individuals to act as maximizing consumers and appropriators, seeking to accumulate the means to ensure their future flow of consumer satisfactions, which meant seeking to acquire property. A system which requires men to see themselves, and to act, as consumers and appropriators, gives little scope for most of them to see themselves and act as exerters and developers of their capacities.[25]

It is market competition as such, not capitalist market relations, that Macpherson is objecting to here.

Now, all forms of an economy based on market relations, and not just the capitalist form, are indeed inconsistent with the developmental ideal in a number of specific contexts. Among them are the holding of incomes at or near minimal subsistence levels, imperialist domination over other national economies, authoritarian control over management decisions, manipulation of political processes in favor of special interests, and inequalities that deny some persons a fair chance to develop their skills, all of which are still with us in varying degrees. Yet in modern times capitalist societies have no monopoly on them, and it is tendentious for anyone to suggest that the so-called socialist societies experience them chiefly because they are at a "lower" stage of economic development.

In short, Macpherson simply has not shown why there cannot be a rational form of "acting as consumers and appropriators" that is perfectly consistent with his own developmental ideal. He never was able to come to terms with the notion that a society based on the developmental ideal, as the natural successor to what has gone before, cannot be something made in the image of "a very old idea," as he put it in a passage quoted above, but rather must be something new and never before seen, a genuine democracy of persons immersed in fully-developed market relations. I shall argue in the concluding chapter that we should accept such a notion.

Conclusion: The Liberal State

When introducing the section on the "Five Themes" above I outlined the liberal state's role as the mediator between the spheres of economics and politics. As noted there, the liberal state historically has allowed contending groups to press their demands for the extension, maintenance, modification, or dismantling of social institutions through structures of party politics and civil liberties that have varied widely in the degree of their dedication to the values of justice and equality, all the while seeking to prevent a fall into overt class warfare and escalating violence.

In his mature period, Macpherson paid more attention to the virtues of the liberal-democratic tradition, and especially to the great importance of the commitment to civil liberties within it, than he had earlier. Just how seriously he took this element is shown in the following passage: "The absence or severe restriction of civil and political liberties must be held, on the ethical [i.e., developmental] concept of powers, to diminish men's powers more than does the market transfer of powers."[26] In view of the intensity of his battle against possessive individualist assumptions, this is an eloquent testimony to his equally strongly held commitment to civil liberties. When he concluded his evaluation of four models of democracy in the last paragraph of *The Life and Times of Liberal Democracy*, he states that his preferred model — participatory democracy — must include "the heart" of the earlier liberal-democratic model worked out by J. S. Mill. And in an essay, also published in 1977, "Do We Need a Theory of the State?" Macpherson announced that he placed himself in a category with "those who accept and would promote the normative values that were read into the liberal-democratic society and state by J. S. Mill and the nineteenth- and twentieth-century idealist theorists,..."[27] So far as I know, this was the first time he ever made an explicit statement of his affiliation, although of course it was implicit in much of his previous work.

We now have all the themes in the social theory of Macpherson's mature period, as well as a sense of the basic ways in which they are internally related to each other. Those interrelationships give his thought a range and solidity that is indeed impressive; I have also sought to show at various points, however, that everything does not quite add up.The deficiency is to be found in the overly restrictive concept of market relations with which he worked throughout his career. In the concluding chapter, I will make the necessary adjustments to his scheme so as to repair that deficiency.

It is also evident that over the entire span of his career Macpherson's thinking comes full circle. For what begins with property and the state in his 1935 master's thesis ends fifty years later — when the major themes from his mature period are sorted out — with a new concept of property that derives its meaning from its function in contemporary political processes within the liberal-democratic state.

4

Canada as a Quasi-Market Society

There is no doubt that from first to last C. B. Macpherson's studies of political theory and practice carried a pragmatic intent: to display the shortcomings of the market-dominated society in which he lived and to show the way to a better one. The foregoing discussion also showed that his dual commitment as scholar-protagonist compelled him to express his advocacy in and through the craft of academic scholarship. This meant that he fully accepted the scholar's responsibility in approaching historical sources, namely that interpretation of the past must be grounded in the mustering of textual evidence, the fair consideration of opposing viewpoints, and a reasoned presentation of his own standpoint.

Macpherson's lifelong project as scholar and protagonist began as an act of personal courage and was performed with tireless devotion and great intellectual ability. In my view, he made a lasting positive contribution to the

practice of academic activity in Canada. In this concluding chapter I wish to accept the legacy of Macpherson's
project, and to do so I will ask how present-day society
appears when it is assessed systematically from the standpoint of Macpherson's core ideas and ideals.

Naturally the answers given will be my own: in no
sense do I claim that this is how Macpherson himself
would have made such an assessment. Indeed, it must be
said at the outset that he would have expressed strong
reservations, if not sharp objections, to some parts of my
sketch. Yet I think that the only appropriate way to accept a legacy such as Macpherson's is to take seriously the
example he set as an epic theorist. This entails not slav-
ishly repeating the answers he gave to the questions he
posed, but rather seeking to do what he did, namely using a critical theory of society to renew and press forcefully a demand for further improvements in the state of
social justice and in the conduct of democratic politics.

Legacy

The distillation in the preceding chapter of the major
themes that run through Macpherson's work reduced them
to two core elements, property and the marketplace. Three
important topics emerged from that distillation, and they
will be taken up again in this chapter; they are the politicization of property, a positive theory of market relations,
and a re-evaluation of consumerism.

One key unresolved issue remains after all of Macpherson's published writings have been considered, namely
whether his unrelenting criticism of market relations and
their social consequences is meant to apply to any and
all forms of a fully-developed market society, or only to
the capitalist type. Of course, in one sense, this is a
hypothetical issue, since so far as fully-developed market
relations are concerned we have actual experience of the
capitalist type only. Yet it is more than that for the nature
and characteristics of non-capitalist forms of a fully-
developed market society are pertinent to an entire range

of public policy choices being faced today by the citizens of many Western nations — and also, in even more dramatic terms, by those in so-called socialist and communist nations. In fact, this may be the single most important point of convergence in global societal change now.

Macpherson gave us an expression that describes this common element now emerging in so many different social formations around the globe: a quasi-market society. So far as I can determine, he used it only once in all his writings, namely, in his 1973 essay "A Political Theory of Property."[1] Intentionally or not, it echoes the phrase "quasi-party system" used in *Democracy in Alberta*. He refers to just two components of this idea, but both are part of the foundations of the quasi-market society. The first, mentioned earlier, is that the marketplace no longer allocates the lion's shares of property rights and the benefits that flow therefrom among individuals and groups. The second is that the state assumes a considerable role in regulating both the economic mechanisms operating in markets and the effects of those mechanisms on individuals and groups. In fact these are largely two different ways of saying the same thing.

Macpherson never made more of the idea than what is in this brief passage; however, in my view his thinking during the last decade would support a much greater role for it, indeed one in which it is the cornerstone of a general theory in political economy, a theory that can grasp the essential factors in an emerging social formation on a global scale. The quasi-market society is basically the same concept as that of the "mixed economy," and it offers a framework within which specific "hybrid" social formations can combine private- and public-sector genes in many different ways. (One good example is Britain's "quango," an acronym for "quasi autonomous non-governmental organization.") In terms of this theory, Canada is seen as already being a quasi-market society or mixed economy, as are also most other OECD nations — that is, Northern, Western and Southern Europe; the United Kingdom, Ireland, and Iceland; North America; Australia, New

Zealand, and Japan: twenty-four in all. In addition, the major socialist nations — the Soviet Union and most of the nations of Eastern Europe — are now (but only quite recently) publicly committed to the same course of development.

The Nature of a Quasi-Market Society

What are the distinguishing characteristics of a quasi-market society? A variety of lists could be constructed; my own emphasizes the integration of diverse institutional forces into a distinctive type of political economy. (1) The public or government sector accounts for about one-half of a nation's annual Gross National Product and about one-quarter of its direct employment. (2) There are fully-developed market relations: labor is a commodity, satisfaction of most needs is accomplished through market purchases, and almost all individuals are engaged in numerous market transactions every day. (3) Notwithstanding (2), the state undertakes indirect regulation of the entire economy and direct regulation of a substantial portion of the national economy. (4) The economy comprises a relatively small number of large enterprises, privately or publicly controlled (or a mixture of both), which dominate the national economy, plus a large number of small enterprises. (5) Income and wealth distributions show large and persistent inequities across sectors of the population. (6) A "welfare floor" protects the least-well-off from being deprived of the basic necessities of life, and in some cases assures a "decent" standard of living.

Whatever the variations in detail among countries might be, these six characteristics are the bedrock upon which the political economy of a quasi-market society is based; and when I want to employ a shortened expression in the discussion to follow, I will refer to them as the "six characteristics." In addition, those countries in which these six features have evolved to the furthest extent also have one other, overriding trait as well: in such countries (e.g., Canada) much of both national and regional political life is taken up explicitly with managing the quasi-market economy, which is thus a form of "political economy" in the fullest sense of the term. There are no major (and very few minor) questions of economic policy that are not by the same token also political issues, and this fact is reflected daily in news reports, journalistic commentary, public opinion poll results, and politicians' attempts to curry public favor.

As the name itself indicates, the marketplace and its activities (characteristic #2 above) are the heart and soul of this emergent social type. Generally speaking, the other five characteristics do not affect the others directly, but rather influence the whole system by operating in and through market relations; this generalization is subject to many qualifications, of course. (A profoundly important "indirect" result is to continuously reinforce and expand the role of market relations in everyday life.) Thus, in describing how its principal features coalesce we should place this characteristic at the center, and arrange the others in orbit around it:

INCOME DISTRIBUTION		WELFARE FLOOR
	MARKET RELATIONS	
CAPITAL CONCENTRATION		REGULATION
	GOVERNMENT SPENDING	

I will illustrate some of the specific interrelationships among these features, as well as how they are mediated by market relations, in a later section of this chapter.

As is the case with any model that attempts to limn the broad outlines of a historically-significant societal type, here too the model captures only what is a general tendency or direction in events at a high level of abstraction. Thus exceptions to the six characteristics will be found almost anywhere one chooses to look. In the end, one must choose either the path that is sometimes derisively called "grand theory," trusting in the existence of the *Zeitgeist* to protect oneself against the consequences of ignoring so much contrary evidence; or alternatively choose the historian's way of approaching the patterns in events by sifting through as much messy detail as one can tolerate. In a book devoted to a practitioner of epic political theory, the former is the more fitting choice.

The first qualification is the theorist's concession to the historian, namely that the great variations in detail cannot be overlooked: the six characteristics refer to a general tendency of historical development, moreover one which is by no means irreversible. First, there are marked differences in levels of economic well-being among countries (say, Sweden and Portugal today) that are quasi-market societies; the generalization will hold — and I think it does — only if one can point to forces at work that will tend to reduce those differences over time. Second, the social consensus that underpins a quasi-market society is strongly affected by periodic swings in popular political ideologies, and those swings are more pronounced in particular countries. The country with the weakest commitment to this consensus is the United States. The United Kingdom under successive Thatcher governments seems determined to destroy it entirely, although ,since in no election has Thatcher's party won an absolute majority of votes, the results should not be interpreted as an affirmation by a majority of the electorate of that ideological agenda. Third, even among those nations where that social consensus is relatively stable, there are wide variations among the ways in which each of the six characteristics — and thus also the resultant mix — is expressed through public policies.

The second qualification is that although many of these

characteristics are also to be found in other countries —
namely in many LDCs (less developed nations) — in addition to those that have been mentioned, LDCs are
(perhaps arbitrarily) excluded from the category of quasi-
market society. This is largely because the majority of their
populations have never been integrated into a wage economy and thus into fully-developed market relations; traditional, pre-capitalist social formations still persist, including
the limited market relations that govern the dealings of
agricultural peasants with a landlord class or with the state.
There appears, however, to be a certain inevitability in the
pattern that will result everywhere, sooner or later, in the
reduction of agricultural laborers to a small fraction of the
working population and the integration of the remainder
into a wage economy of some sort, and in the accompany-
ing transformation in social relations. At present the most
dramatic instance of emerging changes of this kind among
the LDCs is to be found in China.

On the other hand, the Soviet Union, which only in
the summer of 1987 announced its intention to move from
a "command economy" to one in which market relations
will be allowed to operate in a substantial portion of the
national economy, as well as most of the Eastern European socialist countries, are regarded as already being quasi-
market societies.[2] This is because the majority of their
populations have been part of a wage economy for some
time already; because traditional social institutions have
been undermined by official ideologies committed to
"modern" practices; and because those populations have
been heavily influenced (largely through the underground
economy) by Western models of consumerism, well in advance of their capacities to practice affluence. In these nations, fully-developed market relations have been
artificially suppressed by obsolete dogmas, and this is in
the process of being remedied.

One of the most fascinating developments to watch
for in the Soviet Union and Eastern Europe is the evolution of the political consequences resulting from a commitment to expand market relations in their economies.

The introduction of individual and group initiatives and responsibilities into economic relations must lead to intensified demands for the democratization of political life. In Hungary, where the impact of market forces has spread furthest, such demands have been made publicly already.[3] More will follow.

When did the Transition from Capitalism to Socialism occur?

A quasi-market society or mixed economy, then, is one in which fully-developed market relations exist side-by-side with a state apparatus that oversees the national economy and takes responsibility for major social programs through transfer payments. It is neither a capitalist nor a socialist society, but a hybrid form that has some of the features of both. A quasi-market society is "beyond capitalism and socialism." How and when did it come into existence?

To answer this we must first briefly describe its difference from its predecessors with respect to the six characteristics. The ideal capitalist society — which still appears in the fervent rhetoric of "free-market" ideologues — shares three of those six characteristics: fully-developed market relations, extreme disparities in the distribution of income and wealth, and an economic structure in which massive concentrations of corporate capital co-exist with small businesses. The other three are absent as a matter of principle. Public sector expenditures and employment are kept to an absolute minimum (except for military and police functions), as is government regulation of the economy: the role of the state is to guarantee the sanctity of contracts and to provide internal and external security, that is, to protect property. Furthermore, there is no welfare floor, the poor being rescued from misery or extinction only by private charity.

The ideal type of socialist society is just the opposite. The three characteristics inconsistent with "pure" capitalism — a large public sector role in expenditures and employment, overall regulation of the economy, a welfare floor — are meant to predominate in economic planning. Its extreme form is a command economy in which the state plan sets specific performance targets for every producing unit and in which all workers in a real sense are employees of the state. Where differential wages are paid, and the state employees must purchase individually at least some of the important means of subsistence, market relations still prevail, although many major items (housing, education and health care) are effectively removed from the marketplace. The communist ideal envisions the elimination of all market relations and their replacement by a society-wide barter system based on exchanges of direct use-values, that is, a system where neither labor nor goods have prices. The socialist ideal incorporates the institution of economic justice through either an immediate or a gradual narrowing of disparities in income and wealth distribution (including confiscatory inheritance taxes); for communism such differences no longer would be measurable.

Neither of these ideal types has ever existed in reality in full accord with the blueprints drafted by their ideological proponents, of course, although some reasonable approximations are to be occasionally found. Much more interesting than each of the blueprints themselves, when considered in isolation, is the historical tension or dialectical interplay between them.

From the moment of its origins in early modern Europe the development of capitalism was resisted bitterly by most of those affected by it, first in the hopes of restoring the precapitalist social relations that were being destroyed, and later under the banner of the socialist ideal that accepted the radical transformations wrought by capitalism and sought to go beyond them. The opposition began to win significant victories in the most economically advanced nations during the second half of the nineteenth century, especially in achieving legal recognition for trade unions and a gradual extension of the franchise. In most places the "either-or" nature of this contest, that is, the belief on both sides that the paths of capitalism and socialism were divergent, and that there was only a choice between one or the other, without compromise, which has the cast of mind in which Macpherson began his career, persisted into the 1930s. At that point, originating in the Scandinavian countries and spreading to many others after the war, a compromise of immense historical significance was fashioned, resulting in the emergence of the quasi-market society with the characteristics outlined above.

The compromise included an acknowledgement by business interests of a permanent and growing role for the state in the management of national economies and an acceptance of the assumption by the state of major responsibility for social welfare programs. On the other side, it entailed the (largely tacit) acknowledgement by the oppositional forces that there would not be full economic justice in the socialist sense and no significant labor or public control over management prerogatives in enterprises. Both sides accepted the fundamental proposition that major increases in well-being for every social group, whatever its standing on the inequitable income-distribution scale, were to be achieved by general economic growth. This is what was earlier referred to as the "social consensus" that provides the basis for the further evolution of quasi-market societies.

Thus, the question that forms this section heading — "When did the transition from capitalism to socialism occur?" — is misleading (yet just slightly so). In one sense, this "transition" actually did occur, on a world scale, from 1918 to 1949, that is, in the period bounded by the triumph of revolutionary movements in the Soviet Union and China. These and associated events in Eastern Europe and elsewhere meant in effect that capitalist development in the "classical" pattern — e.g., British history from the seventeenth to the nineteenth centuries — would be restricted largely to its countries of origin in Europe and North America, and in modified patterns in other places (such as Japan) where U. S. military power would permit it to occur. No other indigenous copies of this classical pattern are likely to emerge in the future; attempted artificial transplantations of it (which conveniently omit the requirement for liberal-democratic political institutions), for example the current one in Chile, are not likely to survive much beyond the downfall of the repressive regimes that sponsor them.

Since 1945, the dominant political rhetoric outside the circle of OECD countries, by a wide margin, has been either one or another variant of socialism. In terms of a vision governed by a set of ideals, this socialist rhetoric was fashioned primarily out of nineteenth-century European materials, suitably outfitted with a patina of local idiosyncrasies before being broadcast to the population. In almost every case its material basis was to be some version of a command economy in which market relations were strictly confined within a framework of central planning and state-owned enterprises. Yet today most command economies as such are either bankrupt or being dismantled because they cannot provide the conditions for meeting even minimal economic development goals, chief among which is an appropriate motivational context for individuals.

Like its antagonist, therefore, socialism (in its "classical" formulation derived from nineteenth-century European struggles) has already run its course. As originally conceived, its historical mission was to succeed capitalism; its actual mission, however, was to modify capitalism in developed countries and to prevent it from further expansion into other countries during the latter part of twentieth century. As a motivating set of competing ideals, it accomplished this blockage in two ways: first, by forcing the business classes in capitalist nations to accept the compromises that led to the emergence of the quasi-market society; second, through successful revolutionary movements, by preventing the classical pattern of capitalist development from spreading around the world. Adopting Hegelian terminology (always a risky business) here, with apologies to Marx for revising the conclusion to his three volumes of *Capital*, one could say that socialism is the "negation" of capitalism, and the quasi-market society is the "negation of negation."

An objection to this perspective can be lodged from either of two sides. From a certain "right-wing" standpoint, the six characteristics are precisely those of socialism, and therefore countries such as Canada and Sweden already suffer the misfortune of living under that unhappy regime. This is largely a matter of labelling, useful for inspired rhetorical flights but not for much else. One need only reply that, considering such factors as the influence and investment discretion of private capital and the disparities in income and wealth distribution in Canada and Sweden, every one of the great nineteenth-century socialist progenitors would be astonished by such a thought.

From another perspective, some socialist believers could view the quasi-market society as a stepping-stone to the full realization of their dreams. On the basis of the social consensus already determined, in this view only a few additional measures need to be taken, such as a confiscatory inheritance tax, drastic reductions in income inequalities imposed by legislative fiat, and a greatly expanded sector for state-owned enterprises. In reply to this, one can say that the predominant tendency in public policy agendas, even among social-democratic parties, lies in the opposite direction. To be sure, there are still strong commitments to remedying specific ills, such as overcoming pay inequities between men and women and replacing the demeaning welfare apparatus with an entitlement system such as a guaranteed annual income. Once in power, however, every social-democratic government is challenged by the exigencies of managing both divergent group interests and a national economy that is only partly under its direct control (due to its integration within a global setting), all of which tends to restrict its policies and practices within a few degrees of variation around the prevailing social consensus.

OECD Nations as Quasi-Market Societies

As noted at the outset, three issues about contemporary society (politicization of property, theory of market relations, evaluation of consumerism) are of special interest at this point, because in considering them we can utilize Macpherson's legacy to assist us in outlining the main features of a still-developing social type, the quasi-market society. Before turning to these I will provide a sampling of data on the six characteristics; most of the data is about Canada, which therefore offers a case study on the quasi-market society today. Some information pertains to a larger group of OECD countries, thus offering a comparative perspective. The data must only be considered as illustrative, rather than exhaustive or definitive. Moreover, given the great variations in circumstances and political traditions among the twenty-four OECD nations, it is impossible to determine whether or not Canada is "typical" in any of the categories so illustrated. I suspect that Canada now rests approximately at the midpoint on a spectrum — defined by the six characteristics taken as an integrated set — that extends from what is at present the least developed (the USA?) to the most fully developed stage (Scandinavia?) of the quasi-market society. As indicated earlier, the Soviet Union and Eastern European nations should be placed on the spectrum as well, thus producing a situation that has an interesting dynamic tension: The most economically advanced OECD countries have attained the quasi-market society model through capitalism, while others are approaching from an intersecting route, in full flight from largely unhappy applications of an overly rigid socialist ideology.

The data on social and economic conditions in Canada (plus a bit of comparative data) relevant to the six characteristics may be sorted somewhat arbitrarily into two categories: three (public sector economic activity, government regulation of and subsidies to business, and capital concentration) pertain to the societal level of action, and another two (income distribution, and transfer payments and the welfare floor) are relevant on the individual level. While this is convenient for purposes of discussion, in reality the two levels are completely integrated in a unified sphere of social action.

1. Society: Public Sector Economic Activity

A variety of indicators measure the importance of the public sector role in the national economy, including the level of expenditures and capital formation, the relative importance of public sector enterprises, and employment. The materials provided in this section are drawn largely from the work of one of Canada's leading authorities in this field, W. T. Stanbury.

There are reliable measures for total expenditures, by all levels of government ("G") (local, regional, national) in a country, considered as a percentage of its Gross National Product (GNP). The percentage figure in the table below is the ratio of G to GNP:

NATION	%	YEAR
Canada	47.9	1983
United States	38.0	1982
Japan	32.7	1982
United Kingdom	46.4	1981
France	48.6	1981
Germany	47.5	1981
Netherlands	62.5	1980
Sweden*	64.4	1980

*excluding social security payments

Equally significant is the long historical trend for this ratio. In Canada, it rises from between 4 and 7 percent in 1867, to 13.2% in 1913, 15.7% in 1926, 21.4% in 1939, between 22.1% and 26.5% in 1950, between 29.7% and 32.6% in 1960, 36.9% in 1970, and 41.8% in 1980. Therefore, the ratio of G to GNP increased by seven times from 1867 to 1983. The totals include both what are called "exhaustive expenditures," which use up goods and services, and transfer payments between levels of government, and between various governments and individuals; in Canada in 1983, roughly half of total public sector expenditures fell into each of these two categories.

Total government wages and salaries as a percentage of all national wages and salaries was 25.1% by 1977. Public sector employment comprised 23.7% of all employment in Canada in 1975 (24.2% of total public sector employment was at the federal level, 44.4% at the provincial level, and 31.4% at the municipal level). To the 23.7% figure may be added the employment data from public enterprises (see below). Finally as a percentage of the total capital stock in Canada, the share of public capital stock remained at roughly 30% throughout the 1960s and 1970s.

By the early 1980s, the federal and provincial crown corporations that comprise the public enterprises in Canada accounted for a further 5% of GNP, for 4.5% of total national employment, and for 16% of gross fixed capital investment. They include almost the entire range of industrial activity, and are significant in telephone and communications, housing, transportation, power utilities, liquor distribution, and industrial development. Some indication of their relative size is shown by the fact that, among the largest 100 nonfinancial corporations of all types, federal and provincial crown corporations accounted for 14.7% of profits, 17.9% of sales, and 30.8% of assets.

Finally, and in addition to the above, federal and provincial governments in Canada hold equity investments in "mixed enterprises," which are essentially private-sector firms, including minority, equal-share, and majority positions. By the 1980s, there were over 300 significant cases of this type, about two-thirds of which represented holdings by the Federal and Quebec governments. Government investments in mixed enterprises comprised 7.5% of total equity capital in Canada.

If we examine the first indicator (G as % of GNP) as an overall guide to the other components, the massive presence of the public sector in the economic activity of many OECD nations is clearly indicated. The general activities represented by this data, together with the specific regulatory and subsidy apparatus controlling business (see below), both of which have grown steadily in scope over the past century, shows that about half of these modern economies constitute a "zone of exclusion" for capitalist market operations. Given the prevailing political imperatives in these countries, we could further say that the public sector provides the basic framework within which the private sector is allowed to operate now.

Nevertheless, it should be remembered that the end result of most of these public sector activities, so far as their direct impacts on the lives of individuals are concerned, basically serves to reinforce the structure of market relations. This is because their most direct impacts on individuals (as well as their indirect impacts through private businesses), are in one way or another, the provisioning of incomes that are spent through private decisions on goods and services in the marketplace.

The dismantling of certain public sector activities through the so-called process of "privatization," in the United States, the United Kingdom, and by imitation and to a lesser extent in Canada, is in some cases a reasonable response to economic inefficiencies that have been protected from the rules governing other players by the chance outcomes of political influence. In its ideological form, however, privatization does present a short-run challenge to the emerging structures of quasi-market societies. Public support for such ideological constructs, however, tends to wax and wane; I suspect that in the long run the ideological form of privatization will not undermine the basic institutional struts of our mixed economy.

2. Society: Business Regulation and Subsidies

Part of the public sector expenditures detailed above are targeted to services and subsidies by governments to business. A comprehensive review undertaken by the Canadian federal government in 1985 identified fifty-seven major programs and tallied their costs as follows: (1) subsidy programs, direct outlays of $4.5 billion plus foregone revenues (tax expenditures) of $7.7 billion; and (2) service programs, $4.2 billion in costs, for a grand total of $16.4 billion.[5] The major outlays and tax expenditures — for which no comparable total figures are available — of the ten provincial governments must also be added. Since 1970, total expenditures of all types by provincial governments have been almost equal to total federal expenditures; on the assumption that provincial spending on services and subsidies to business was the same proportion of all expenditures, the $16.4 billion figure could be double.

So far as regulation is concerned, Stanbury notes that it is pervasive in the fields of transportation, energy, insurance, banking, securities, telecommunications, broadcasting, agriculture, and the professions. He cites a study that counted 1,744 federal and provincial regulatory statutes in effect in Canada in 1978, and he estimates that about 30% of gross domestic product manufacture was subject to direct regulation.

In this category of activity, therefore, we find both financial and nonfinancial support for and "interference" with the operation of markets on the part of governments. By these means, and others, elected governments possess the instruments to respond quickly to public pressures and to fulfill social and economic objectives that are not being achieved by the "uncontrolled" process of market forces. Earlier comments about privatization applies equally to the current "deregulatory" thrusts: they are unlikely to greatly affect the underlying foundations of the mixed economy.

3. Capital Concentration

The long-term trend toward concentrated ownership of private sector industrial and financial assets continued apace while the public sector role was expanding dramatically during the post-1945 period. In Canada, the total number of industrial firms increased from thirteen to eighty-three thousand from 1946-1976; the proportion in the total of the top 70 firms dropped from 0.55% to 0.08%, but the top 70 maintained their 50% share of total assets.

A line graph in W. K. Carroll's book, *Corporate Power and Canadian Capitalism*, shows the remarkable consistency in the structure of capital concentration in Canada over a thirty-year period from 1946 onwards.[6] Over this period, the line showing the share of industrial assets controlled by the top 70 industrial firms, as a percentage of all industrial assets, shifts by less than 10% above and below the fifty-percent level; in 1976 it is almost exactly at the same point it was in 1946. There is no reason to suppose that there have been significant changes since 1976.

The concentration of asset control in the Canadian financial sector is even more marked: in 1976 the top 20 firms controlled assets worth twice as much as the total assets of the top 70 industrial firms, and the top five out of that twenty controlled about two-thirds of the total assets of financial companies.

Much has been made of this capital concentration from a variety of perspectives. I will mention only one aspect that is directly relevant to the foregoing considerations, namely that this concentration is an important part of the ongoing "co-operative tension" between the public and private economic sectors in a quasi-market society. The public sector is itself highly concentrated (in Canada for example, eleven governments), and thus the interactions between the agents for these two clusters of economic and political power can be performed in a reasonably "efficient" manner. This is an appropriate way of effectively managing a complex and dynamic domestic system (which is also integrated into a global system) where authority is shared *de facto* between those who stand at the pinnacle of private sector economic interests, on the one hand, and of regional and national political power, on the other.

4. Individuals: Income Distribution

In a market-oriented society cash income is the determining factor in access to most goods and services for all
individuals. For most persons the single most important
source of income is wages and salaries; transfer payments,
investment income, and capital gains are other significant
sources. Struggles to enact minimum wage levels, and efforts to maximize rates of pay through collective bargain-
ing, have been at the center of relations between capital
and labor since the beginning of the Industrial Revolution,
and indeed in most OECD nations real wages have risen
steadily over time throughout the period of industriali-
zation.

Although the campaign to win wage levels that assure
some decent standard of living has been successful, little
if any change has occurred in the proportionate distribution of incomes across various sectors of the population,
at least during the period when any reliable statistical data
is available. This distribution has remained remarkably stable, for example, over the last fifty years (that is, during
the period of welfare gains after the Great Depression and
the sustained rise in real incomes after 1945). This means
that the economically-stronger sectors of the income earning population have managed to maintain their *relative*
shares of income (and presumably of wealth) virtually intact, although it is sometimes alleged that the "welfare
state" is dedicated to the radical redistribution or even
levelling of income and wealth. General increases in well-
being, therefore, can be attributed to the rising level of
wealth in the society as a whole (in Canada mean real income has more than doubled since 1945), which carries
all sectors upward while holding their relative shares pretty
much constant.

Certainly there are some net redistribution effects from
government welfare policies, and thus some other measure, such as "command over resources," would be (at least
in theory) a better measure than income shares are of the
end-point relative standing of different groups in a given

society. Nonetheless, such more general measures are evidently difficult to construct. The leading Canadian authority in the field, Irwin Gillespie, has written: "During the 15 years under consideration [1961-1976], governments have been unsuccessful in increasing the degree of redistribution from the rich to the poor such that the 'share' of command over resources of the poor has increased significantly."[8]

A very small sample of the abundant statistical data on income distribution is given below.[9] (In the following section special note of the importance of transfer payments in the cash incomes of the various sectors will be taken.) The data are usually reported in the form of "quintiles," that is, the percentage of total national income received by each one-fifth of the population, when the whole income-receiving population (families and unattached individuals) is ranked from the lowest to the highest income recipient. Thus the first quintile represents the lowest 20% of the population; the second quintile, the next 20% (i.e., those who rank twenty-first to fortieth), and so on to the fifth quintile, representing the top 20% of all income recipients.

CANADIAN DATA: INCOME SHARES BY QUINTILE

Year	First	Second	Third	Fourth	Fifth
1951	4.4	11.3	18.3	23.3	42.8
1961	4.2	11.9	18.3	24.5	41.1
1971	3.6	10.6	17.6	24.9	43.3
1981	4.6	10.9	17.6	25.2	41.8
1984	4.5	10.3	17.1	25.0	43.0

COMPARATIVE DATA*

Country	First	Second	Third	Fourth	Fifth
United States	4.4	11.5	16.9	24.0	43.2
Sweden	4.6	10.5	15.9	23.6	45.4
United Kingdom	6.4	11.7	16.5	23.4	42.0
France	2.3	7.7	13.3	22.0	54.7
Germany	5.3	9.5	12.8	17.5	54.9
Japan	5.6	11.3	16.0	12.6	44.5
Australia	7.1	12.9	17.6	23.5	38.9

*for various years in the 1960s

The Canadian data indicate the stability over time of the income shares, and it is representative of a common feature in the economically-advanced OECD countries. The comparative data show the rough similarity across such countries, although there are interesting variations. Indeed, so uniform is this pattern that some authorities refer to a "4-40 rule," that is, about 4% to the lowest quintile and 40% to the highest.

5. Transfer Payments and the Welfare Floor

In addition to interest on the national debt (which is, in Canada's case, mostly income to its own citizens), transfer payments by the federal government represent disbursements to individuals, subsidies and capital assistance, as well as intergovernmental transfers. Fully three-quarters of national government expenditures are transfer payments now (as opposed to exhaustive expenditures, that is, purchases of goods and services), which generally demonstrates the size of the financial "reshuffling" function of governments that maintains adequate levels of money flows in the economy.

At this point, I am concerned mainly with the significance of transfers for individuals, which include cash payments made directly to individuals, of three main types: general programs (welfare, income supplements, workers' compensation, and unemployment insurance); programs for the elderly, including cash transfers such as OAS and tax expenditures such as RRSPs; and programs for families, such as family allowances and the child tax credit. Here too the dimensions of the activity are relevant: transfers comprised fully 27.2% of *all* personal income in Canada in 1983, more than double the proportion of thirty years previous. The other type is comprised of support programs for health care, housing, and schooling at all levels; about 60% of transfer expenditures fall into this category. In 1981, total transfers of all these types constituted 18.9% of GNP.

Naturally the poorest persons derive the greatest benefits from transfers, although all income groups benefit to some extent, especially from the universal programs such as health care and education. The importance of these transfers in providing a welfare floor for the poorest sector is shown in the comparison of income shares by quintile with and without their impact on incomes (Canada, 1981 data):

	First	Second	Third	Fourth	Fifth
Income before Transfers	1.4	9.6	17.8	26.4	44.9
Total Money Income	4.6	10.9	17.6	25.2	41.8

Thus transfers more than tripled the money income share of the poorest quintile, while having a small (in some cases negligible) impact on the remainder.

The five characteristics on which some selected information has been given are all part of a dense web of functions in contemporary society; in other words, they play a part in many aspects of social action, only one of which is the institutional makeup of a quasi-market society. For example, massive public sector expenditures and government management of the economy reflect a political commitment to securing general social well-being, which is intended to ensure a standard of living for everyone at some minimal level of decency, regardless of income-earning potential. (Of course this commitment, when translated into policies and practices, is often insufficiently strong in particular times and places to prevent some persons from falling into poverty and degradation.)

My special interest, however, is in how these five characteristics support and enhance the centrality of market relations in everyday life. Public sector expenditures, both exhaustive and transfer, maintain high levels of money flows in marketplace transactions for both individuals and firms, and also account for between one-quarter and one-third of all employment, the cash incomes from which are also translated into market purchases. Regulation and subsidies amount to policy-directed control over businesses, but they are also an alternative to systems in which governments attempt to produce goods and services (rather than policies) directly, and in this sense they reinforce market-oriented structures of behavior. In addition, the high level of capital concentration facilitates a kind of partnership between big government and big business, with the partners seeking to manage jointly their national economies through effective responses to domestic and international market forces. All these macroeconomic and macropolitical manipulations keep market relations fixed firmly in place in the everyday life of most individuals, whose daily routines are absorbed in a rich mixture composed of both real and vicarious experiences of buying and selling.

Three Issues

The basic concept of a quasi-market society is this: dominant institutional forces (the alliance of concentrated economic and political power) place market relations at the center of social action, while also constraining marketplace operations within boundaries set by political events. Those boundaries shift constantly in response to the ebb and flow of political currents, but they are permanent enough to allow the clear distinction of this form of political economy from any others where a relatively unrestricted play of market relations prevails. So far as the lives of individuals are concerned, the quasi-market society perpetuates severe inequalities in the distribution of income and wealth, while providing, by its welfare floor, sufficient resources to enable most of the poorest persons to avoid absolute deprivation.

Let us recall once again Macpherson's criterion for a political theory worthy of its heritage, which he enunciated at the outset of his career in his essay "On the Study of Politics in Canada" (1938): Political theory can provide a "principle of unity" for the discipline of political science when it focusses on "the interaction of political ideas and concrete political facts." The concept of the quasi-market society that has been developed here, I submit, is plausible as a contribution that satisfies this criterion.

This elaborated notion of a quasi-market society remains faithful to Macpherson's two core themes, property and the marketplace. There are, however, a number of points in my elaboration which, if accepted, require that revisions be made to the prescriptions that Macpherson derived from his treatment of his two themes. These revisions become apparent in a consideration of three issues: the politicizing of property, a positive theory of market relations, and the evaluation of consumerism.

The quasi-market society represents a thoroughgoing politicization of property, which offers our contemporary society a clear alternative to either the socialization of property (the familiar socialist demand) or unregulated capitalism. The process of politicizing property leaves by far the greatest and most desirable portion of economic wealth in private hands, usually in starkly unequal portions. At the same time, the possession and enjoyment of this wealth — with respect to both its totality and its relative shares — are subject ultimately to control by democratically-elected governments. Some minimal redistribution of command over resources occurs through the application of public policies, but far more significant is the impetus for increasing overall well-being (in unequal shares) through sustained economic growth, by means of an almost countless number and variety of political manipulations of market forces.

This course appears to have the firm support of the vast majority of citizens in the OECD countries. In specific terms, this means an affirmation of the two opposed but complementary sides of a quasi-market society: on the one hand, a market-oriented economy in which private sector businesses take most of the initiative in economic development; on the other, a political economy in which democratic governments exercise an overall supervisory and management role in the economy, stepping in routinely to adjust the outcomes of the operations of market forces. There are broad swings of public policy and opinion regarding the relations between the zones of private and public sector initiatives, but in most cases this managerial role of governments is exercised irrespective of political ideology (that is, whether liberal, conservative, or social-democratic). At various times in most OECD countries in the post-1945 period liberal, conservative, and social-democratic governments alike, responding to the imperatives of the moment, have found themselves promoting both types of initiatives.

To say that property has been "politicized" is of course to concede that it has been indirectly socialized. In other words, the process involving the politicization of property recognizes the rational core in the socialist objection to capitalism, namely that modern economic wealth results from the general application of human technological ingenuity of all types, irrespective of the legal fiction of ownership or control over the means of production. It also recognizes that all who participate in the creation of this wealth should be guaranteed some minimum share of benefits that will permit them to enjoy whatever is regarded as a "decent" standard of living according to the prevailing criteria.

Nonetheless, the program for the politicization of property also concedes the rational core in the capitalist objection to socialism, namely that a modern industrial economy simply cannot function according to an authoritative allocation (by public bureaucracies) of productive inputs and of the resultant economic wealth.

It also concedes that, to date, the program of economic justice in states nominally committed to socialism and communism has been in practice an outrageous sham, such that persistent inequalities in the command over resources in those states rival those in managed capitalist societies.

Politicizing property means steering an erratic course between the Scylla and Charybdis of "pure" capitalism and socialism. The quasi-market society avoids the intolerable polarization of great wealth and equally great poverty inevitably produced by unregulated capitalism; it also avoids the unsatisfying combination of egalitarian rhetoric, privileged elites, and sclerotic productivity that has been perfected by those states nominally dedicated to the ideals of socialism and communism.

The upshot is that quasi-market societies are founded on a positive theory of market relations. By this phrase I mean that there is an explicit commitment to market forces as an indispensable mechanism for assuring an acceptable level of economic performance (measured by indicators of real overall growth, increases in productivity, and so forth) in a modern economy. This is largely because the complexity of this economy, in terms of the sheer number of types of inputs, products, and processes, as well as the dynamic state of international markets, is such that it simply cannot achieve acceptable performance levels through any known form of centralized planning. Partially regulated market forces, which permit continuous adjustments in resource allocations through innumerable individual decisions by producers and consumers, can yield a better result than centralized planning can, but only with close supervision by governments. Furthermore, only the system of market-type benefits appears to supply sufficient motivation for most individuals to develop and exert the full range of their abilities.

Nevertheless, *this commitment to market forces in a quasi-market society is purely pragmatic rather than ideological*, which is what differentiates it from the theory and practice of "pure" capitalism. The centrality of market relations for public policy and everyday life obtains only as long as an adequate level of collective and personal benefits is delivered thereby. Every instance of significant market failure or relative disadvantage, whether occurring internally in a nation or in international trade, even in the notorious bastions of "free enterprise" in the United States (witness the proposed trade protection laws), is greeted with loud demands — by business, labor, and other interests alike — for compensatory political action.

Managed capitalist societies have found their way to the quasi-market form by gradually circumscribing with political authority the domain of market forces. As noted earlier, the Soviet Union and the Eastern European nations are now proceeding into it along an intersecting route, by gradually withdrawing bureaucratic control from various economic spheres, allowing them to fall partially under the sway of market-based determinations. Obviously, this is a purely pragmatic decision. What is still unclear is the extent to which the proponents of this dramatic change in direction are aware that they will be unable to contain its secondary consequences, especially the inevitable dispersal of market-oriented modes of behavior throughout the interstices of collective and personal life.

The positive theory of market relations deviates in other ways from the critique of capitalism exemplified in Macpherson's work. The most important of these has to do with the relation between the spheres of work and consumption. Perhaps the single most distinctive principle to which all the great theorists of socialism adhered, from the mid-nineteenth-century onwards, is that by its very nature capitalism destroys the possibility of deriving satisfaction from labor for the great majority of the industrial workforce. Therefore, a cornerstone of socialism was the restoration or achievement of satisfaction in labor in one way or another (for example, in the utopias of Fourier or William Morris). The largely hidden premise in this outlook was that labor was the single most meaningful venue for human satisfaction in general. This point was often made by denigrating other domains of satisfaction, particularly that of consumption. We earlier discussed how

Macpherson represented the stark opposition of the domains of doing (active development and enjoyment of human powers) and consumption (purely passive and meaningless activity).

There are undoubtedly many individuals for whom finding work that is intrinsically satisfying (which includes decent working conditions, of course) is a high priority. This should not be surprising; however, there is no evidence that any significant portion of individuals see this objective as a "political" or ideological matter, that is, as part of a larger struggle for radical change in existing social institutions. Nor is there any evidence that such persons see their pursuit of satisfying work as somehow inconsistent with the structure of market relations; quite the contrary, they find that enhancing their own market power is a very effective way of accomplishing this objective. Seeking satisfying work is one of a series of interconnected goals, along with others like a high income, sufficient leisure time, and good family relations, and individuals are inclined to try to achieve the best "package" they can with respect to all of them as a set.

The positive theory of market relations deviates most sharply from the received socialist critique, as exemplified by the work of Macpherson and others, in the evaluation of consumption activity. Basing itself primarily on the concepts of false needs and false consciousness (and especially on reification and commodity fetishism), this critique made two allegations. First, that individuals are systematically misled in looking for gratification in consumer purchases by what are only apparent or superficial need-satisfactions, rather than genuine ones; in other words, consumer decisions in a market-oriented setting are almost entirely irrelevant where the issue is how truly human needs may be satisfied. Second, the deception of apparent need-satisfaction prevents individuals from detecting the real sources of their oppression (which are lodged in the relations of production) and thus from striving to transcend the system of market relations as such.

This critique was always largely a speculative exercise,

for little evidence of any kind had ever been offered in support of the deception or manipulation hypothesis. The abundant evidence we do have from marketing and consumer behavior research is that on balance consumer experiences represent *for the most part* the genuine gratification of quite genuine and deeply-felt needs. Naturally many specific dissatisfactions or disappointments are sensed, and there are surely expressions of desire that are either illegal or unacceptable according to prevailing community standards. It can even be maintained that efforts by individuals to match the objectives of their wants to the characteristics of goods can be difficult or impossible in some cases, due to the number and complexity of marketplace transactions in a fully-developed market society. Nevertheless, none of this proves that most individuals are deceived by the "propaganda of commodities" (especially by advertising claims) into making systematic errors about the *entire* assortment of their wants or the means for satisfying them.

Since there is ample room for misunderstanding here, I would like to state explicitly that no attempt is being made here to share the fantasy of free enterprise ideologues who regard the system of market relations as the Eighth Wonder of the World. I am only indicating that there is no special kind of defect in them by comparison with other systems, either pre-capitalist or utopian socialist in nature. Every kind of economic order may be pervaded with injustice, and in every known society individuals and groups have prevented themselves, at least in part, from realizing their own objectives by constructing behavioral patterns and pictures of the world that contain inconsistencies and regressive features. The quasi-market society is not immune from contamination by this longstanding practice.

As indicated earlier, all of the principal features of the quasi-market society reinforce the centrality of market relations in the everyday life of most individuals. The general rise in real incomes over a century of industrial development, as well as the existence of the welfare floor, have drawn almost everyone deeply into the experience of being a consumer on a daily basis for the entirety of one's life. During the past half-century considerable amounts of daily personal time have been shifted from other types of activities to intensive involvement in all aspects of the act of consumption. Many studies of consumer behavior confirm that this is regarded as a voluntary choice and for the most part is thought to be both stimulating and enjoyable.

The genuine gratifications derived from consumer experiences are of two kinds. There are those flowing from the sheer proliferation of goods and their complex characteristics, for our tendency to surround ourselves with layers of objects seems to be a basic human trait; this is the "materialistic" aspect of market-oriented behavior. The other is a playful indulgence in the circulation of images attached to objects, to the point where every act of consumption appears to be only a fleeting expression of a purely evanescent order, a walk in the kingdom of fairies (to borrow the appellation that Hobbes bestowed on the religious establishments of his day); this is its "symbolic" aspect.

It is the symbolic aspect that is most potent in luring individuals into full involvement with acts of consumption. This is because in marketing and advertising imagistic modes of communication are used to establish a dense web of connections between the characteristics of goods, on the one hand, and the vast range of known motivational impulses that are at work in the individual's search for satisfaction, on the other. For most persons at least, in no other dimension of life — such as work, education, or any other — is an attempt made to connect so intensively and pervasively the individual's motivations with the possibilities of gratification in the surrounding social environment. Therefore it is certainly no accident that the sphere of consumption should have a special value in a quasi-market society. It is quite possible to imagine also that this may change in time, with some other dimension of life assuming the position of priority that consumption now enjoys; as yet we have no sign of it.

The institutional network of the quasi-market society

(combining the six characteristics), as it exists at present in advanced OECD countries, shows an explicit bias for promoting consumerism as the single most important zone of gratification in the lives of individuals. There seems to be little question that, as the nominally socialist countries follow their own paths to the quasi-market society, there too the bias towards consumerism will be promoted by the authorities. Nevertheless we should note two qualifications. First, the consumerist bias occurs not in isolation, but within a larger context where — for most OECD nations — very important domains of life, especially health care and education, but often including others, have been removed almost entirely from the sphere of market-driven consumer decisions. This has happened due to strong and persistent demands by the majority of citizens. It would be quite incorrect to think therefore that all domains of personal life are absorbed in market relations now or that this is likely to happen in the future.

The other qualification is that quasi-market societies are dynamic rather than static types of societies. This means that changes — perhaps dramatic ones — in collective and personal behavior are bound to occur over time. In particular, although some structure of general market relations must persist out of necessity, for purely pragmatic reasons, the existing consumerist bias need not be regarded as our unalterable destiny. People may eventually become jaded with the consumption of images and give greater priority to other sources of satisfaction. If so the utopian theorists like Macpherson will have their day.

Epilogue

An Appreciation

At the time when he accepted his first university teaching appointment at the age of twenty-four, C. B. Macpherson had settled upon his vocation, his ideological standpoint, and his mission. So far as the first-mentioned is concerned, there is no evidence that he ever considered any other path for himself save that of a university teacher and an author of scholarly publications. So far as his political ideology is concerned, every page of his master's thesis shows his passionate commitment to socialism, in a form defined essentially by the nineteenth-century European working class movement; that commitment stayed with him undiminished in intensity thereafter. Finally, his very first published essay as a young academic, "On the Study of Politics in Canada," announced what was to be his life's mission: to cause the academic discipline in his own country, in which he wished to participate, to recognize and accept the value — indeed the necessity — of an approach to political theory that was grounded in a commitment to radical social improvement.

What Macpherson had not yet found at the onset of his career in 1935, and what he was not to find until he was almost at mid-career, was his own distinctive "voice." The term "voice" refers to an appropriate mode of expression for his ideas, one that combined a personal writing style with a fully-developed and highly original interpretive thrust — the voice that speaks clearly in *The Political Theory of Possessive Individualism* and thereafter. To be sure, all that came before constituted a preparation for the breakthrough that occurred in his maturity. But until the late nineteen-fifties he had not succeeded in satisfactorily articulating through his scholarship the results of the synthesis he had achieved early in life for himself, in his own mind, between his ideological commitment and his mission as a member of the academic profession.

Until approximately 1955 those two aspects of his being subsisted together but separate in an uneasy alliance. His ideological commitment was unshakeable, and was allowed to show through most of his scholarly writing in varying degrees. For example, it is clearly evident in the journal article that represents his first foray into the subject matter that later would make him famous, "Hobbes Today" (1945), as well as in the conclusions to *Democracy in Alberta* (1953). At times it seems to veer towards a somewhat dogmatic Marxism before being harnessed again. As indicated above, Professor Macpherson's status as a Marxist of some sort is debated in the secondary literature. Undoubtedly, he was always "sympathetic" to Marxist theory; but neither the substance nor the citations in his writings indicates that he read very widely in Marxist literature, nor did he ever *systematically* confront the fundamental concepts debated in that literature, such as class consciousness, proletariat, alienation and reification, capitalist economic crisis, and surplus value. The rather diffident responses he gave in an interview published in 1983, dealing with his assessment of Marx, are symptomatic of the uses to which he put the Marxist tradition in his publications.[1]

Nevertheless, the extent to which Macpherson sympathized with Marxism is not the most important issue regarding the writings of his formative period. The important point is that before the late nineteen-fifties he had not succeeded in completely integrating the two sides of his dual commitment as scholar and protagonist. What I mean is simply that in the end his ideological commitment got in the way of his treatment of his subject-matter, resulting in an only partially satisfactory interpretive exposition. The interpretation in "Hobbes Today," for example, is based on wholly unsupported, allusive comments about the nature of "bourgeois society." In addition, the conclusions to *Democracy in Alberta* rest on a tendentious theory of social class and class consciousness, for Macpherson's position is riddled with unclarified assumptions about the existence of a self-conscious "working class" and about the relation between social group consciousness and social being.

Nonetheless, with the concept of "possessive individualism" Macpherson discovered the tool that finally would enable him to unite scholar and protagonist successfully and indeed brilliantly. Since it was centered on the workings of fully-developed market relations, this concept could draw into itself (as the related notion of acquisitiveness had for R. H. Tawney) all the central concerns in the traditional socialist critique of capitalist society. Therefore it served well — as Macpherson testified in his concluding section of *Possessive Individualism* — the cause of his ideological commitment.[2] On the other hand, whether or not other established scholars agreed with him, this concept had a completely plausible relation to the actual textual evidence in the history of liberal political thought that he was examining. Thus, he could express the substantive concerns that motivated his ideological commitment "inside" the very stuff of scholarly debate, so to speak. He had found the principle of unity he had been seeking for a quarter of a century.

Other interpretations of Macpherson's work very different from the one advanced here undoubtedly can be made.[3] Fair enough. Many of those already advanced, however, especially by authors who profess to share Macpherson's kind of commitments, exhibit a common fault: they ignore his dedication to serving the purely academic side of political science as a discipline throughout most of his career. In the nineteen-thirties and -forties he worked out his sense of mission in studies on the history and development of his discipline in Canada. He poured out a continuous stream of book reviews in his field, on a range of subjects much wider than his specialty of political theory alone. In the nineteen-fifties he did comprehensive assessments of the development of political science on the international plane, and in the nineteen-sixties he undertook many obligations of a purely professional sort.

It is my contention that one cannot understand Macpherson's career and thought unless one appreciates this aspect of his activity. His desire to assist in the realization in Canada of the traditional socialist program for social change was not formulated independently of his choice of an academic vocation; rather, those two aspects of his life appear to have emerged simultaneously and to have remained intertwined thereafter. Each aspect nurtured the other and caused it to evolve and mature. It is because he took so seriously his role as a scholar that he continued to search for his own voice, and it was the sustained effort involved in that search that finally resulted in the great books of his mature period. Nor was he any less devoted to his commitment as protagonist, and that dedication too drove him on until he found the interpretive scheme that would accomplish his mission of renovating his academic discipline. In my view, it was this fertile and uninterrupted interaction between the two aspects that is responsible for the enduring significance of Macpherson's life and work.

NOTES

I am greatful to Oxford University Press for permission to quote from the work of C.B. Macpherson.

1

1. Sheldon Wolin, "Political Theory as a Vocation" pp. 1078-81.

2. *The Rise and Fall of Economic Justice* 53.

3. Herbert Marcuse, "The Struggle against Liberalism in the Totalitarian View of the State" (1933), in *Negations* 3-42; Max Horkheimer, "Egoismus und Freiheitsbewegung" (1935), in *Kritische Theorie* II: 1-81.

2

1. This section is based upon an interview with C. B. Macpherson by the author, Toronto, 2 July 1986. During this interview CBM directed me to his master's thesis and graciously gave me permission to quote from it.

2. *Canadian Forum*, June 1932, 332; *Pacific Affairs* 25 (1952), 96-7; *Spectator* 195 (Sept. 9, 1955), 327-8 and succeeding issues.

3. For his wartime views see especially *Reflections on the Revolution of our Time* (1943) and *Faith, Reason, and Civilization* (1944); cf. Macpherson's comment on the latter in *CJEPS* 40 (1945), pp.310-11.

4. On Kay Macpherson see June Callwood's article in the *Globe and Mail*, 25 November 1987.

5. Thesis p. 14.

6. Thesis p. 8.

7. Thesis p. 86.

8. Thesis p. 115.

9. Thesis p. 91.

10. Thesis p. 129.

11. Thesis pp. 214, 215.

12. Thesis p. 232.

13. Thesis p. 295.

14. Thesis p. 240.

15. *The Rise and Fall of Economic Justice* pp. 16, 119.

16. Thesis p. 308.

17. Thesis pp. 309, 320-1.

18. Review of Pareto's *General Sociology*, in *CJEPS* 3 (1937), p. 470.

19. "On the Study of Politics in Canada" pp. 159, 161.

20. *Ibid.* 164.

21. Review of Smith, *Public Opinion in a Democracy,* in *CJEPS* 6 (1940), pp. 116-7.

22. "The History of Political Ideas," *CJEPS* 7 (1941), p. 564.

23. "The Meaning of Economic Democracy" pp. 403, 404.

24. *Ibid.* p. 409.

25. *Ibid.* pp. 420; 404; 417.

26. "The Position of Political Science" pp. 457-9.

27. "Hobbes Today" p. 525.

28. "The Deceptive Task of Political Theory" p. 199.

29. *Possessive Individualism* p. 271.

30. "The Political Theory of Social Credit" p. 390.

31. *Ibid.* p. 393.

32. *Democracy in Alberta* pp. 20; 58; 100.

33. *Ibid.* pp. 218ff.

34. *The Canadian Forum*, January 1955, p. 224.

35. *Democracy in Alberta* p. 225.

36. *Democracy in Alberta* p. 249.

37. "On the Study of Politics in Canada" p. 164.

3

1. Victor Svacek, "The Elusive Marxism of C. B. Macpherson" p. 419.

2. *CJEPS* 29 (1963), p. 562.

3. *Possessive Individualism* pp. 4; 53-4; 48 (author's italics).

4. *Democratic Theory* pp. 182-3; 193.

5. Letter to the author dated January 13, 1980.

6. *Life and Times* p. 2; *Rise and Fall* p. 100.

7. *Rise and Fall* pp. 56; 62.

8. Marx, *Grundrisse* pp. 409-10; 79.

9. Marx, *Capital* I: p. 772.

10. Stanley Moore, *Marx on the Choice between Socialism and Communism.*

11. *Democratic Theory* pp. 4; 54-5.

12. *Ibid.* pp. 9; 74-7; 4-5.

13. *Ibid.* p.30.

14. *Ibid.* pp. 34-5.

15. *Ibid.* p. 51.
16. *Life and Times* pp. 62; 70.
17. *Ibid.* pp. 91-2; 99; 102; 115.
18. *Democratic Theory* p. 94; *Rise and Fall* p. 41.
19. *Life and Times* pp. 102-7.
20. *Rise and Fall* p. 51.
21. *Democratic Theory* pp. 121-3; 131; 137.
22. *Rise and Fall* pp. 83-4.
23. Steven Lukes, "The Real and Ideal Worlds of Democracy." p. 120(1).
24. *Life and Times,* p. 2.
25. *Ibid.* p. 61.
26. *Democratic Theory* p. 14.
27. *Rise and Fall,* pp. 56, 62.

4

1. *Democratic Theory* pp. 133-4.
2. *Globe and Mail,* June 27 & 30, 1987.
3. *Globe and Mail,* February 4, 1988.
4. W. T. Stanbury, *Business-Government Relations,* ch. 3; J. L. Howard & W. T. Stanbury, in: G. Lermer (ed.), *Probing Leviathan,* ch. 4 and Appendix.
5. Government of Canada, Task Force on Program Review, *Services and Subsidies to Business* p. 1.
6. W. K. Carroll, *Corporate Power and Canadian Capitalism* pp. 64-71.
7. F. Vaillancourt, *Income Distribution and Economic Security in Canada,* Table 1-7 and pp. 11-12.
8. S. Jain, *Size Distribution of Income,* Table 2. W. I. Gillespie, *The Redistribution of Income in Canada* p. 171.
9. Vaillancourt 1-58 *passim,* esp. Tables 1-5 & 1-19. Stanbury 51-3.

Epilogue

1. Interview with CBM by Frank Cunningham, 1983.
2. Possessive Individualism 162 equates "bourgeois society" with "possessive market society."
3. See, e.g., D. Drache and A. Kroker (1987).

LIST OF WORKS CITED

I. Works by Crawford Brough Macpherson *(in chronological order)*

NOTE: The *Canadian Journal of Economics and Political Science* is abbreviated *CJEPS*. Titles of the books reviewed by Macpherson are provided in Victor Svacek's bibliography.

1935   "Voluntary Associations within the State, 1900-1934, with special reference to the Place of Trade Unions in relation to the State in Great Britain." Thesis submitted in partial fulfillment of the requirements of the MSc(Econ) degree, The London School of Economics, April 1935.

1936-7 Book reviews in *New Frontier*, April 1936 [George Seldes], May 1936 [H. M. Tomlinson], and January 1937 [V. I Lenin et. al.].

1937   "Pareto's *General Sociology*," *CJEPS* 3: 458-71.

1938   "On the Study of Politics in Canada," in: H. A. Innis (ed.), *Essays in Political Economy in Honour of E. J. Urwick*. Toronto: University of Toronto Press. pp. 147-65.

1940   Book review [C. W. Smith Jr.] in *CJEPS* 6: 116-7.

1941   "The History of Political Ideas," *CJEPS* 7: 564-77.

1942   "The Meaning of Economic Democracy," *University of Toronto Quarterly* 11: 403-20.

1942   "The Position of Political Science," *Culture* 3: 452-9.

1943   "Sir William Temple, Political Scientist?" *CJEPS* 9: 39-54.

1945   Book review [Harold Laski] in *CJEPS* 9: 310-1.
        Book review [William Haller & Godfrey Davies/Don M. Wolfe] in *CJEPS* 9: 633-6.
        "Hobbes Today," *CJEPS* 9: 524-34.

1949   "The Political Theory of Social Credit," *CJEPS* 15: 378-93.

1951   "Locke on Capitalist Appropriation," *Western Political Quarterly* 4: 550-66.

1952   Book review [Sraffa's and Dobb's edition of Ricardo] in *Western Political Quarterly* 5: 673-4; also 7 (1954): 287-94 and 8 (1955): 639-40.

1953   *Democracy in Alberta: The Theory and Practice of a Quasi-Party System*. Toronto: University of Toronto Press. Republished in 1962 by the University of Toronto Press with a revised subtitle, *Social Credit and the Party System*. The 1962 edition has been cited in the text.

1954   "The Social Bearing of Locke's Political Theory," *Western Political Quarterly* 7: 1-22.
        "L'Enseignement de la science politique au Canada," *Revue francaise de science politique* 4: 384-400.
        "The Deceptive Task of Political Theory," *Cambridge Journal* 7: 560-8.

"World Trends in Political Science Research," *American Political Science Review* 48: 427-49.

1955 "Democracy in Alberta: A Reply," *Canadian Forum*, January 1955, 223-25.

1957 "The Social Sciences." In: J. Park (ed.), *The Culture of Contemporary Canada*. Ithaca: Cornell University Press, pp. 181-221.

1958 "Political Science." *Encyclopedia Canadiana*.

1962 *The Political Theory of Possessive Individualism: Hobbes to Locke*. Oxford: Oxford University Press.

1963 "Scholars and Spectres: A Rejoinder to Viner," *CJEPS* 29: 559-62.

1973 *Democratic Theory: Essays in Retrieval*. Oxford University Press.

1977 *The Life and Times of Liberal Democracy*. Oxford University Press.

1977 Editor and contributor: *Property: Mainstream and Critical Positions*. Toronto: University of Toronto Press.

1983 Interview with Frank Cunningham, *Socialist Studies/Etudes Socialistes*, No. 1, pp. 7-18.

1985 *The Rise and Fall of Economic Justice*. Oxford University Press.

II. Works by other Authors

Canada. Task Force on Program Review. *Services and Subsidies to Business*. Ottawa: Supply and Services Canada, 1986.

Carroll, William K. *Corporate Power and Canadian Capitalism*. Vancouver, B.C.: University of British Columbia Press, 1986.

Drache, Daniel and Kroker, Arthur. "C. B. Macpherson, 1911-1987." *Canadian Journal of Political and Social Theory*, Vol. 11 (1987), pp. 99-105.

Gillespie, W. Irwin. *The Redistribution of Income in Canada*. Ottawa: Institute of Canadian Studies, Carleton University, 1980.

Horkheimer, Max. *Kritische Theorie*. Edited by Alfred Schmidt. Frankfurt: Suhrkamp, 2 vols., 1968.

Howard, John L. and Stanbury, W.T., "Measuring Leviathan." In: George Lermer (ed.), *Probing Leviathan*. The Fraser Institute, 1984.

Jain, Shail. *Size Distribution of Income: A Compilation of Data*. Washington, D.C.: The World Bank, 1975.

Kontos, Alkis, ed. *Powers, Possessions and Freedom: Essays in Honour of C. B. Macpherson*. University of Toronto Press, 1979.

Laski, Harold J. *Faith, Reason, and Civilization*. New York: Viking Press, 1944.

————. *Reflections on the Revolution of our Time*. New York: Viking Press, 1943.

Lipset, Seymour Martin. *Agrarian Socialism* [1950]. New York: Anchor Books, 1968.

————. Review of *Democracy in Alberta*, *Canadian Forum*, November 1954, 175-7 and December 1954, 196-8.

Lukes, Stephen. "The Real and Ideal Worlds of Democracy." In: A. Kontos (ed)., *Powers, Possessions and Freedom*, pp. 139-52.

Marcuse, Herbert. *Negations: Essays in Critical Theory*. Translated by Jeremy Shapiro. Boston: Beacon Press, 1968.

————. *An Essay on Liberation*. Boston: Beacon Press, 1969.

Marx, Karl. *Capital*, Vol. I. Translated by Ben Fowkes. London: Penguin, 1976.

————. *Grundrisse*. Translated by Martin Nicolaus. London: Penguin, 1973.

Moore, Stanley. *Marx on the Choice between Socialism and Communism*. Cambridge, Mass.: Harvard University Press, 1980.

van der Sprenkel, Otto B. Articles in *Canadian Forum*, June 1932, p. 332 and *Spectator*, September 1955, pp. 327-8.

Stanbury, W. T. *Business-Government Relations in Canada*. Toronto: Methuen Publications, 1986.

Strauss, Leo. *The Political Philosophy of Hobbes*. Oxford: Oxford University Press, 1936.

Svacek, Victor. "Crawford Brough Macpherson: A Bibliography." In: Alkis Kontos (ed)., *Powers, Possessions and Freedom*, pp. 167-78.

————. "The Elusive Marxism of C. B. Macpherson," *CJPS* 9, 1976: 395-422.

Tawney, R. H. *The Acquisitive Society* [1921]. London: G. Bell, 1952.

————. *The Agrarian Question in the Sixteenth Century* [1912].

————. *Equality* [1931]. New York: Capricorn Books, 1961.

————. *Religion and the Rise of Capitalism* [1926].

Vaillancourt, Francois. *Income Distribution and Economic Security in Canada*. Collected Research Studies, Royal Commission on the Economic Union and Development Prospects for Canada, Vol. I. Ottawa: Supply and Services Canada, 1985.

Viner, Jacob. "Possessive Individualism as Original Sin," *CJEPS* 29: 548-59 and 562-4.

Wolin, Sheldon. "Political Theory as a Vocation," *American Political Science Review* 63, 1969: 1062-1082.